RECOVERY? GOAL ON!

A book about Life Coaching and Recovery from Mental ill Health

By

Humphrey Greaves

Professional Life Coach

And

Service User

Copyright Humphrey Greaves 2013

Foreword

> A Professional Life Coach and NLP Practitioner has had his own Coaching Practice called Humphrey Greaves Coaching Practice since 2002. Humphrey started Life Coaching at Southwark Mind, he particularly specialised in working with the Kindred Minds project, a black and minority ethnic project within Southwark Mind. Humphrey offers free six sessions although he may give up to 12 sessions in some cases.

As a mental health service survivor, activist and manager of Kindred Minds (a Black and Minority Ethnic user-led, user run project based within Southwark Mind) I feel very privileged to be writing the foreword to this exciting new book by Humphrey Greaves.

I first met Humphrey on a Personal Development training course in South London. Humphrey was already trained as a life coach, and from the first time he spoke his passion about life coaching shone through. It was clear that life coaching had been a life-line for him and he wanted to offer it to others. We quickly discovered that we had a lot in common – we both wanted to let the world know that there are alternatives to what is prescribed through the mental health systems and each of us was on our own adventure of communicating these ideas. Humphrey made a strong impression on me initially, and even more so as I got to know him better when we worked together as colleagues at Southwark Mind. He is a very down to earth person with a deep sense of quietness that knows there's more to what is generally just seen or heard. He is in touch with the small details, and has a friendly and pleasant way of connecting with people, in a way that makes people feel relaxed and above all has a very positive and hopeful attitude. "Why put your dreams on hold – you can do it!"

But as I slowly learnt, this had not always been the case and he had faced numerous challenges in both his personal and professional life, ending up in the psychiatric system on mind-numbing medication and little prospect of recovery. Then he was offered life coaching, and this literally became his life-line, enabling to have dreams of a hopeful future and work towards achieving them. Life coaching was already being used in business and other environments, and Humphrey became keen to adapt/develop such methods as a tool of personal recovery for people who have, like him, experienced extreme mental distress and often unhelpful/damaging 'treatments' within mental health settings and been categorised as unable to recover or achieve success in life. He therefore trained as a life coach and, drawing on his own and others personal experience, developed the method of life coaching described in this book that has enabled many people, especially those with a psychiatric diagnosis, to move towards building a hopeful and compelling future. I had a great opportunity to see this happening first hand when we established and worked together at Kindred Minds where Humphrey introduced his method of life coaching as a free service to mental health service users. It soon became clear how much potential such life-coaching had, since it genuinely enabled people to take more control of their lives by identifying their own personal goals and working towards them in holistic ways.

Humphrey is now letting others be witness to his pioneering work too, by writing about his experience as a life coach in this exciting new book. Here, he describes his philosophy and how he has used and adapted the GROW model of life coaching for working with people whose life has often been taken over and controlled by the mental health system.

This book challenges the old adage 'once a psychiatric patient, always a psychiatric patient' and, through its focus on real life people and situations conveys a real sense of optimism and inspiration. Making it essential reading for users of mental health services who have too often had their potential, hopes and dreams crushed as a result of their mental health problems and unhelpful treatments in services and stigma and discrimination by society at large. In addition, this thought-provoking book is essential reading for those who work in both statutory and voluntary sector organizations, since it provides guidance and practical tools that can be used to ensure life coaching is a genuinely empowering process led by service users and not just another service-led psychiatric intervention.

As someone who has had their own often challenging journey through the mental health system, I have learnt much from Humphrey Greaves and his empathic and empowering way of working. With this book he adds to his already significant contribution to the mental health service user literature. 'Building a Compelling Future' and 'Circle of One' chapters in the book called Mental Health, Service User Involvement and Recovery, 2010, Jessica Kingsley). His use of his own personal experience, skills and talents, his realistic positivity and his commitment to putting the person and their own dreams and aspirations first serves as an inspiration to us all.

Renuka Bhakta
January 2012

Recovery? Goal ON!

Chapter 1
Objection your honour, don't call me lazy!

Chapter 2
Why I wrote these chapters on Life Coaching and Recovery

Chapter 3
Why put your Dreams on hold?

Chapter 4
What is Life Coaching?

Chapter 5
Helpful qualities that makes a good Coach?

Chapter 6
Recovery or Bust

Chapter 7
Ask the Coach – questions and answers

Chapter 8
Service User in the Driving seat

Creating Future History

Write your own Epilogue!

Chapter 1

Objection your honour, don't call me lazy!

Many people still see people who use Psychiatric Services as deluded, crazy, mad, screaming whilst running through the wards of the Asylum. Despite the Mental Health act 1983. Community Care and after the non occurrence of Armageddon, once we were all let out of Psychiatric Hospitals, this notion still prevails and is anything but eased by modern day Politicians. Who seem to refer to us Service Users as Economic parasites. Don't believe me? Look at the papers, watch the News. Very seldom are we valued or appreciated. Anyway, I will leave such comments for now.

In fact, I am no angel, I have many faults. One of them was to agree in conversations that patients of Psychiatric Hospital could not survive in the Community. That is despite having spent up to 6 months in such a Hospital and having acquired the diagnosis Schizophrenia in 1981. To make matters worse I was a living example of someone living in the Community. What an idiot! you might say. That's true, but part of that was because, particularly in the 1980's the medical profession were very slow to explain things, if at all. So we had very little to go on.

Nevertheless, when I started to get better, back in 1981, the thought of staying in Hospital for ever terrified me. Yet I was gulping down this nonsense that people with Mental illness could not live in the community. It is surprising how obedient we are to Professionals and the authorities, in fact we often put more trust in their opinions and theories than the average Joe. Even when they declare certainty; when perhaps in their heart they are not sure. For instance I knew of Psychiatric patients who had gone back to the community and coped, yet I still followed, I was basing my opinions on old information, myths, etc. Though I stood as a living example; as someone with Schizophrenia living in the community. Besides the real question was, not whether Service Users could live in the community but whether they would get sufficient support to do so?

Be careful what you believe it may come to pass!

Very often in life we come to believe Scientists, Politicians, Health Professionals etc. However, sometimes there is a sleight of hand, meaning sometimes that some things are hidden from us. Sometimes because of the passage of time or modernisation. What do I mean?

Well I studied History at School, the 1st and 2nd World Wars. I admit I was not very bright and perhaps not diligent enough to read up on Sir Winston Churchill's Life History. But then do most ordinary people? Anyway, when I was out of Psychiatric Hospital and applying for job after job. If I had known that Sir Winston Churchill suffered from Manic Depression yet still helped to save the World, that sure would have given me some hope, as I am sure it would have given lots of Service Users both yesterday and today.

I would have felt more able to stand up to employers who did not feel I was up to the job I would have told them about Sir Winston Churchill, mind you that may have got me sectioned! Yet to my knowledge the media who blatantly highlight our ill health e.g. "Bonkers Bruno" or Cricketer Mark Trescothick's Mental ill Health supposedly being exposed by his England Cricket Coach, the media never happen to mention that Service Users do have a positive role to play e.g. Winston Churchill. Instead I was left feeling life is over.

Today after many years we have Celebrities like Ruby Wax, Stephen Fry, Frank Bruno, talking about their Mental Health and joining the "Time to Change" campaign to combat stigma.

Question: It is great what the Celebrities do and I would like to give a heartfelt thank you to all of them. However, why has it taken so long for the Government and the media to show more than limited support for the Service User trying to Recover from Mental illness?

Moot point, how come they never show or tell of Celebrities who have overcome Schizophrenia who are able to manage their illness? Is it because there is too much stigma around Schizophrenia? How would a Service User in the work place manage?

THOUGHT BUBBLES!

Pick up your bed and walk!

"You're not ill you're a layabout."

"Excuse me Sir who diagnosed me as ill? And by the way did I not have to have a Medical Certificate/Report to say I could not work, that entitled me to these benefits?"

"And by the way give us a job?"

"What's that? You do not think much of my Health record?"

Having told Service Users, rightly or wrongly, that they cannot work, Politicians are now saying, when all is said and done, that they have to work or their benefits will be cut. Now I know there are ifs and buts etc. but that for me is the bottom line. Having ruined countless Service Users lives, excluded them from Society, they now want to send them to work. Not because they care but because we have burned a hole in their pocket. In other words we are an Economic black hole, its costing them too much to keep us on ice. I ask again, who said we were ill? Who do the Medical Profession work for? Who is their boss? The Government? Who set the criteria in the first place? Lest it be forgotten a lot of Service Users were brought in against their will, kicking and screaming, saying they were not ill, before they were baptised with a Mental Health diagnosis.

Where are the jobs?

It's not me sir. It's him!

That aside, I am not criticising either the Medical Profession or Governments of the day as such. I am just giving a taste of what it feels like to be harassed and harangued, every time there is a crisis, in a way that says that the Service User is the cause of the crisis. We, the Service Users always seem to be the scapegoats for the Nation's ills.

What about Transition?

Sometimes I have a recurring nightmare. It goes like this: I go to bed in my flat, but when I wake up I am in a red hot Arabian Desert miles from anywhere. This holds many different meanings for me. When I was ill in 2000 I was worried that my family and I would end up homeless. Similarly, Service Users worry about how they will manage and where they will live, if their benefits are cut and if they are unable to find work or feel they cannot cope with work.

If you are a Mortgagee, picture for a moment the interest rates on your Mortgage increasing by 50% and your income being unable to match this sudden increase. Or maybe you lose your job and have no income, then imagine you are no longer able to work in your Profession or Trade. Suddenly things don't look too good do they? Anyone can end up being a User of Mental Health Services within a blink of an eye, many will loose their families, friends, houses, employment etc. You know how I know? Because it happened to me! One in four people will experience mental ill health at some time in their lives.

There needs to be a period when Service Users can regain their confidence, perhaps retrain, and recover emotionally not just physically. This period I call the transition period. When someone becomes ill they should, I believe, be given help to make the transition from Mental illness - to Recovery - to the Society in general. Part of being in the Society in general might include returning to work. But I shall talk about this later.

Chapter 2

Why I wrote these chapters on Life Coaching and Recovery

My name is Humphrey Greaves, I have been using Mental Health Services since 1981 with approximately 4 admissions to date at the time of writing. My last admission being 2000 that's 10 years ago. I was firstly diagnosed with Schizophrenia, more recently I have been re diagnosed with Severe Depression. Today, I am a Professional Life Coach and Neuro Linguistic Practitioner (NLP) being self employed since 2002 as a NLP Practitioner and Life Coach.

Surplus to requirements.

There have been been many turning points along my life, a highly significant one was when I learned relaxation in 1991 in Milton Keynes Hospital and another is my journey as a Life Coach. Basically, when I trained to be a Life Coach in 2003 -2004 I was deeper than rock bottom. Myself and my wife were headed for Divorce, I had lost my home and step children and was trying to recover from Mental illness, having been in a Mental Health Hospital in 2000. Yet, during the Life Coaching training, I learned to Coach and gained a new sense of purpose in my life.

Suddenly I had a new sense of purpose with a new outlook, this was remarkable, since most of the Coaching was done by my fellow trainee Coaches as we practised on each other during the course. Many of them had no Psychological or Personal Development background, yet the transformation was amazing. I had arrived feeling hopeless and left the course like a man on a mission.

Here I am now, talking about the future, I discovered I still had dreams, goals, things I wanted to contribute, and new things I wanted to try. I am not saying I do not take medication, because I do and it, for me, is a helpful tool, likewise so is Life Coaching a helpful tool. I use Life Coaching to discern what I want to do, be, or have in my life. Sometimes the Mental Health Service is so bent on fixing and curing you, they do not seem to know what the Service User is being fixed for! Now that seems a strange thing to say doesn't it? Moot point: "If my life has been a living hell and you fix me and put me back in the same situation I tried to escape from, without giving me the tools to cut a new path through life, where is the sense in that? Of course it is likely I may become broken and need fixing again, hence the revolving door syndrome.

Stephen Covey author of the book "7 Habits of Highly Effective People" published by Simon Schuster UK Ltd (1989) Page 40 wrote:

"The way we see the problem is the problem …….. And their immediate request is key to revealing their basic paradigm. "How do you do it? Teach me the techniques." What they are really saying is, "Give me some quick fix advice or solution that will relieve the pain in my own situation."

They will find people who will meet their wants and teach these things; and for a short time, skills and techniques may appear to work. They may eliminate some of the cosmetic or acute problems through Social aspirin and band aids.

But the underlying chronic condition remains and eventually new acute symptoms will appear. The more people are into quick fix and focus on the acute problems and pain, the more their approach contributes to the underlying chronic condition. "The way we see the problem is the problem."

What do the words from Stephen Covey mean, and how does it fit in with Life Coaching and Mental Health?

Exercise

I want you to try a simple exercise when you read Stephen Covey's passage here, where the words say they or their etc. I want you firstly to substitute the words Service User as you read through the passage. Then secondly, I want you to substitute the word Mental Health Profession for words their and they etc.

I think you will see at least 2 different views to the same problem, try it.

Observation point

There are two points I want to make on the Stephen Covey passage, one is that Service Users must be given more quality time by Professionals and be listened to, which will eventually save time and money. Since taking time to get to know what the individual wants, needs, and their goals; in other words to get to know them as human beings, may make all the difference and solve the revolving door syndrome.

Too many people are on the other side of the road, when that is not the side they would have chosen. There used be a comedy sketch where an old lady would be standing by the roadside when a well meaning Boy Scout, who was passing, takes the old lady to the other side of the road without asking whether she wanted to cross the road or not. Angry, she starts to hit the Boy Scout with her umbrella, for she had just spent the last half hour crossing the road, now she will have to do it all over again!

Secondly, by substituting the words they, and their with the words Mental Health Professional you will see the problem through different eyes. However, if you substitute the word Service User instead of the words they, and their in the Steven Covey passage you will see the problem from a different angle.

ASK?

I feel that Life Coaching could be an aid to Mental Health Professionals and Social Workers etc. Not least because it turns on its head the question what can I do for you? Which is often the question asked by Professionals to, "what do you want to do with your life? What are your goals? And what are you the client or Service User prepared to do to achieve your goals?

Life Coaching, in my experience, can be used to help those nearing Recovery from Mental ill Health to focus on the next stage in their lives. There are some Recovery Models about, such as in Social Inclusion and Recovery by Perkins and Repper (2006), but each individual can design their own Recovery Model. What is Recovery for one person, may not be Recovery for another. Ultimately, it should be the Service User's decision. I see Life Coaching not as part of the cure for Mental ill Health, but the Recovery of the Service User from Mental illness. Helping him or her to take part with the rest of Society.

TRANSITION IS A LIVE WIRE!

I also wrote these chapters because nobody ever talks about transition from Mental ill Health, to the Service User, reclaiming their place in Society. E.g. if you have been out of work for 5 years due to ill health, though you may now have recovered enough to contemplate going back to work. The mere thought of returning to work can sometimes lead to anxiety and thus a possible relapse. If you, the reader, can remember when you were last on leave for say a fortnight or off work sick for a while, did you notice the changes when you got back? Was your desk in the same place? Had you been moved to another Department? Had some old colleagues left and been replaced by new recruits? Had the procedures at work changed? Will you need new training? Or will you have to start a completely new job?

It is all very well saying the Service User ought to work, and that they are work-shy, because some new policy has been devised or some new theory expounded. Think about the Service Users journey; and also consider that when Politicians and the like, roll out some new program, Service Users are unlikely to have been part of that process. By this I mean the Research, Planning etc. I know various charities like Mind and Rethink try to keep Service Users informed and there are some Service User Consultations. However for the most part, the first most Service Users hear of changes is either on the News or in the Newspaper, usually after some rhetoric about Service Users being scroungers and bleeding the Economy. Remember the Service User may not have been part of the thinking process for these policies and may find them threatening, the policies may have the potential of being their worst nightmare.

It is time Society worked with Service Users instead of Stigmatising them, like an unwanted mess in the corner. It is my humble opinion, if you want the best out of people you encourage them, you do not berate them and put them down. Although I have spoken mainly about employment, because that is what Society is concerned about most at the moment, other areas such as Housing etc. could equally be included.

I believe the Service User can be part of his or her own care and they can also be part of their own future! It is important to listen to service Users' dreams and goals and where possible to encourage them to achieve them. You might see a whole new outlook if Service Users knew they had a future too!

Chapter 3

WHY PUT YOUR DREAMS ON HOLD?

I would like to read a short passage to you:

"It is up to you! Whose dream is it anyway?

Everyday we are bombarded by tales of so called famous people who have done this or that e.g. Footballers, Pop Stars, Scientists, Billionaire Business men, Actors, Actresses and so on. I bet you could name a few. Go on name a few. How about Oprah Winfrey or Tina Turner or Wayne Rooney, or Bill Gates or Richard Branson or Alan Sugar?

Well they are important I guess, but then so are you. It is time to think of you. Your Dreams, your hopes, your skills and talents that are a part of you, and how you can use them to do things you want; or to help you reach your goals. Why not? So long as you are not harming yourself or others. Why put your Dreams on Hold?

If there is something you really want to do, start working towards it now. Even if it is just planning it in your mind, I use the following phrase as my self starter "tomorrow is my today." When I find myself putting things off I remind myself of this saying. I always used to put things off, it was always live my Dreams tomorrow, I will do it tomorrow: then like me you wake up, and the time has passed.

So, Why do I mention people like Bill Gates? Most of the people I mentioned did not wait for permission to live their Dreams or listen to the doubters who said it could not be done. No, they took the chance that they might fail. They took the chance that their friends might laugh at them. Despite it all they took a chance on their Dreams, they took a chance on themselves.

Bill Gates went to a top American Educational Institution called Harvard, people all over the world would give anything to study there. What does Bill Gates go and do? He drops out. Just think of his fellow students who might have thought he was crazy, Could you imagine what you would say if you were his parents.

Yet nobody laughs now! Microsoft is the top computer company in the world , think of the courage it must have taken to not only follow his Dream but to keep following his Dream.

What about Tina Turner? In her book "I Tina Turner" Tina Turner tells of her life when she was abused and beaten by her husband Ike Turner, this happened even after they had become world famous Pop Stars. They were known for songs like "Nut Bush". Yet Tina Turner ran away from Ike without claiming her share of her wealth from Ike that they had earned together. Nevertheless she followed her Dream, she became a top selling solo female artist. She sang such songs as: "What's Love got to do with it", and "Simply the Best".

Why do we like to hear about famous people? Because they are often living their Dreams.

Why Put your Dreams on Hold?

You don't have to be famous to live your dreams, you do not have to be rich or powerful.

Take for instance Martine Wright, she was just an everyday person going to work ,coming home, going to work, you know the routine. Then the 7/7 bombings happened. Martine lost both legs. Devastation. In the Evening Standard Newspaper 26th April 2006, Martine Wright appears in an article with a photograph showing her false legs listing some of her Dreams "I want to walk, run and fly a plane."

In the News of the World News paper 4th May 2008 an article again appeared this time showing Martine Wright the blushing Bride having walked 42 steps to marry her sweetheart.

I ask you again **Why Put Your Dreams on Hold?**

Think about that question Why Put Your Dreams on Hold? For a moment, then think of how Society through the ages has stolen Service Users' dreams, often through detainment in Asylums, removal of sections from the Brain, imprisonment, even death. How they condemned the Service User.

Imagine what its like to be asked "if you were guaranteed success what would you do, be, or have?" Just imagine how refreshing that might be to have someone interested in your feelings and see what your view of your future is, not some pre-designed plan, where you have to fit into some authorities' plan or theories.

They are both difficult questions: "Why put Dreams on Hold?, and "if you were guaranteed success what would you do be or have?" The Life Coach or other Practitioner does not know what the client is going to say. That's the whole point in asking them!

The Service Users' experience can sometimes be a gloomy one, filled with loneliness and despair. We often face exclusion from Society or we have to cleverly hide our pain on a daily basis. That is why when I saw the Medical Profession talking about the importance of "hope" to the Service User, my first thought was: "I thought that is what they were supposed to be doing?" I have never known anyone go to any kind of Doctor seeking gloom and despair, one is hoping for good news and hope for the future, otherwise why go to the Doctor? Secondly, I thought, "it is about time, at last they are considering the Service User and that we need hope too!" I refer to the Recovery model as per Perkins and Repper *Social Inclusion and Recovery: A Model for Mental Health Practice(2006).*

The Recovery model as proposed by Perkins and Repper highlights "HOPE" as being one of the important elements of their Recovery model. Which endears the model to the author's heart, as I am also a Service User. Hope can make the difference between life and death, between sickness and health, this applies to general medicine too! Why did we miss the importance of hope in Mental Health Medicine until now?

Whoever told you to stop dreaming, did you a great disservice!

I went to school in the days where, if you were caught day dreaming, you would be rudely awakened by the thud of a board rubber which has just missed your head, leaving a white after-burn of chalk dust. You would look in the direction of the teacher who had launched this missile, only to see him scowl saying "stop Day Dreaming".

Yet virtually every man-made thing started off as a Dream or idea, look around you, maybe a group of people put their ideas together, e.g. the mobile phone, the computer, the washing machine, the chair, the clock, the watch, the telephone etc. Sometimes ideas and Dreams have been passed down through the ages, e.g. Leonardo De Vinci's Parachute, was not developed until centuries after his death. Is someone who is day dreaming really wasting their time?

Exercise

Look around you and notice how many man-made things are around you, then. find out, if you can who first thought of it and reflect on the power of a dream or an idea.

Then reflect on how you as a Professional, handle the Service User's Dreams and ideas and try to reflect on the power of ideas. Think of Edmund Mount Hilary's Dream to be the first man to climb Mount Everest or Bill Gates' Dream to put a Personal Computer on the desk of every office and every home. A few years ago that was thought to be impossible, nobody laughs now.

I suggest that Professionals handle the Service User's Dreams with care, because these very dreams could be the power-pack that powers the Service User to good health. Think about it, what would cause or power a man to climb Mt Everest? What would power men in to space, it is not just about money, American Billionaires have gone into space via the Russian Space program, and as far as I know had chosen to, when they could have carried on living quite comfortably on earth; if you will, but paid to go up in space. It was because they had always dreamt of doing it!

If we could harness the dreams, hopes and desires of the Service User, so that they get to to do the things they want to do; they are more likely to become more motivated to look after their own health, thus aiding their recovery. It's not rocket science.

I contend we are more than just a collection of chemicals, each one of us has that something special that makes us unique. You can't plot that on your computer; what I am suggesting is Society should not write people off, because they do not fit into Society's desired outcomes, much of which are artificial anyway and vary according to which theory is used to define it. Man will, in my opinion, never be able to predict the future. We can calculate probabilities maybe, but not the future.

Exercise

Can you think of something you have written off as impossible in the past, yet today you see it happening? List 5 things.

Consider this below:

JUST WHEN WE THINK IT IS IMPOSSIBLE WE ARE INTERRUPTED BY SOMEONE WHOSE DONE IT!

Things they said were impossible, yet done in my life time:

1) *The Berlin Wall coming down so East and West Germany could be unified.*
2) *I know it is a cliché these days but man landing on the Moon.*
3) *Heart transplants, I can remember watching the News as a boy and thinking the idea was so silly. Heart transplants are almost routine these days.*
4) *Sailing round the world single handed*
5) *Borg winning Wimbledon 5 times in a row.*
6) *People talking on mobile phones*
7) *That there would be a Woman Prime Minister of the U.K.*
8) *That personal Computers would be on the desk of virtually every office in the world*
9) *That President Obama would be the first Black President Of the United States of America*

Just as you have seen, just as we think it is impossible, we are interrupted by some one who has just done it.

So I would urge Professionals not to crush Service Users' Dreams "You never know there may be something in it." Let each person write their own Life script and strive for their impossible dreams!

Chapter 4

What is Life Coaching?

There are many different types of Coaching you can explore the different types of Coaching in a book called "How Coaching Works: the essential guide to History and practice of effective coaching by Joseph O'connor and Andrea Lages (2007) published by A&C Black London.

The word "Life" in Life Coaching means personal Coaching as opposed to, say, Corporate Coaching for instance.

The definition of Coaching, which I like, is one used by Myles Downey in his book called Effective Coaching (2003) published by Thomson.

Myles Downey writes: *"Coaching is the art of facilitating the performance, learning and development of another."*

Let's look at some of the words used in that definition:

1) "Performance": this means to improve the performance of a specific task or specific goal.
2) "Development": this means personal growth and greater self awareness.
3) "Facilitate": implies that the person being Coached has the capacity to think something through himself, to have insight or a creative idea.

Examples where Life Coaching is used today.

Life Coaching is being used in Business, Finance, Sales, Careers, Motivational Coaching, Stress Reduction, Management, in the National Health Service for Management. And so on.

Dilys Jones and Peter Murphy in their manual: "Introduction to Coaching for Health and Social Care" (2007) Published by Pavilion, encourages Health and Social Care Management to use Coaching as a developmental tool both for small groups and individuals. I thought to myself WHY NOT USE LIFE COACHING TO EMPOWER SERVICE USERS?

Why I think: Life Coaching can be used to empower Service Users.

I suggest that Life Coaching can be used to empower the Service User whilst in Recovery; since to use it whilst the Service User is in crisis, would, I suggest, be unhelpful. If you picture Coaching as a muscle builder, for it to work the ligaments and sinews must be in place first. Coaching could be the bridge that enables transition by aiding Recovery and enabling Service Users to work towards their own goals.

Life Coaching does not rely on diagnosis, like Clinical Psychology or Psychiatry in fact Coaching was developed with healthy people in mind. My argument is that, when I Coach, I am not trying to cure Mental illness, in fact, I am trying to encourage the Service User to think about and work towards their own goals, which they hope will enable them to join the wider community.

Imagine you had a domesticated Lion Cub and you wanted to re introduce it to the wild. If you were a Zoo Keeper would you just leave it in the wild one day to fend for itself or would you gradually ease it back into the wild, having seen that it has the skills to survive?

Sometimes, when a Service User is so keen to get out of Hospital, they give no thought as to how they are going to survive, by this I mean Mentally survive. There is often a feeling of; I will be o.k. Once I get out. The question that needs, I feel, to be asked is: what do you, the Service User, want to do with your life? Put in a less threatening way: "If you knew it was guaranteed and you could have anything, what would you do, be, or have? In short, you are asking what the Client/Service User wants.

THE GROW MODEL.

One of the cornerstones of my practice of Coaching is based on the Grow Model. As a Coach I can simply use the Grow Model to form structure and focus to my conversations with my client during our sessions. The words G.R.O.W. are an acronym for **Goal. Reality. Options. Willingness to act.** Myles Downey describes the Grow model in his book "Effective Coaching" (2003) Please note Myles Downey uses the term "Wrap up" for the W. in the Grow Model I prefer Willingness to act. The G.R.O.W model gives the suggested order of questions asked by the Coach.

G. = Goal

I generally ask my client / Service User what Goal they would like to work towards and achieve. Sometimes the Service User has difficulty choosing a specific Goal. So I try to widen his or her panoramic view e.g. by saying: "If you knew you could have anything and you were guaranteed success, what would you do, be or have? Notice I do not ask them what they feel they can achieve, as often our feelings are coloured by retrospective Guru's hindsight is always 20/20 vision or Societies cocktail of know-it-alls predicting the result before the Client/Service User has had a chance to plot his or her course.

It is for this reason that I ask the Client/Service User to look at what they would really like to do, rather than labour on what Society thinks they should be doing. Sometimes, by doing this one thing they can open doors that actually gives them a new sense of purpose.

To date, I have never had a Service User say they want to win the Lottery or be a Millionaire, either through my personal development groups called "Building a Compelling Future" or in any of my Life Coaching sessions so far.

Neither do I discuss their diagnosis, because I want to know what their hopes and dreams are. I want them to have the opportunity to explore their hopes and dreams and think about what they would really love to do with their lives. My Coaching practice Motto is:

WHY PUT YOUR DREAMS ON HOLD?

I then encourage them to be more specific about what it is they would like to work towards; taking a wide view first is better than making assumptions. For instance, because someone is good at something or has done it in the past, does not necessarily mean they want to do it. Sometimes we may say to ourselves, I do what I do, because this is all I know, or I do this because I have always done it.

My submission, and this through personal experience, is not doing what you would really love to do "can damage your health" whilst doing what you like can help in restoring or at least get a foot-hold on it, by working towards something you would love to do. Despite Society's anxieties the result of working towards something you love, will actually aid Society not harm it. In his book called Unconditional success (2002) published by Bantam Books, Nick Williams writes Pages 112 - 113:

"Our gifts need to find a home, by being brought to the light of day and being shared with the world, and our work can be the way in which we bring our gifts to the world, and make our soul visible."

I try not to prejudge my clients/Service Users, since I do not know what they are capable of, my role is to be as non judgemental as possible. Contrary to stigma often levelled at Service Users, we are often very skilled and very knowledgeable and come from all different walks of Life. One cannot always tell just by looking!

However, I contend that I do not need to know the client's diagnosis, since I am not medically trained and if I am told by the client/Service User that they suffer from Depression or Schizophrenia etc., their Diagnosis does not tell me the degree to which a person is ill anyway, as people function at different levels.

R = Reality

Reality, this is the Client/Service User's Reality. I encourage them to focus on their current resources, this will include skills, people they know, tools, etc. In relation to their chosen goal. Though sometimes it may involve considering old skills etc. from the Client/Service User's past. Again it is not about judgement or looking behind the Client/Service User's words, it is about listening to what they have to say and working with what they present. As their Coach I am not their Therapist or Psychiatrist, I am not above them but I work along side them.

O = Options

Here we explore the Client/Service User's options, choices and possibilities. This is where Coaching changes up a gear, since often Service Users are restricted by both their Mental ill Health or Society or simply their own circumstances. An example of their own circumstances might be that they are going through Divorce, this may have affected their health or may cause them to be homeless.

Looking at options often brings the sweet aroma of hope, by looking at possibilities, instead of what they cannot do. It is here that there is a major link between the Recovery Model (Perkins and Repper) and Life Coaching.

Let's suppose a Service User was a van driver and is given a medication by their Psychiatrist for Depression. Let's also suppose that this medication is prone to making the recipient drowsy plus the recipient is likely to be on the medication for a long time. This means effectively that the van driver has probably lost their job, their family may be dependant on their income, they may be able to retrain, but that may be sometime in the future. It is possible they may lose hope. Questions like what do I do for a living? Come to mind, imagine how refreshing it would be if one can look at what is possible rather than the negative.

W = How willing are you to act.

It is all right coming up with options but the Client / Service User has to decide what they are prepared to do, to make their goal a reality. I call this their willingness to act, another way of putting it is, are they willing to pay the price? Being willing to pay the price does not usually refer to money but what they are prepared to do to make it happen!

As Coach I use a simple Scale of 1 -10 asking them how willing they are to act. 1 = low and 10 = high. If, for instance, a client says for example 5. I as Coach might say what will make it a 10, or if they are really not interested in pursuing that option, we have at least eliminated it and are able to work on something they do want to do!

That is a brief outline of the Grow Model the above description is not meant to be exhaustive but I describe it the way I use it.

IT'S THAT SIMPLE!

The GROW Model can be learned and used within a short space of time and is operational almost immediately. The Grow model is transparent to the extent that the client can easily follow what the Coach is doing, no reading behind the words or chasing smoking mirrors. No! The client takes the Coach where he or she wants the Coach to go, in other words the Coach follows the client's interest. Sometimes the client simply wants to explore possibilities, as a Coach one should leave the door open, you just never know what a Client is capable of.

COACHING IS ECONOMICAL.

Coaching is economical because it is easy to learn, as it is a skills based learning. You do not need a PhD to use it. The cost of training is within easy reach of most organizations. When Coaching is used as part of the Service User's Recovery, helping them to make the transition back into the community, which may include taking the first steps to returning to employment, I believe it will increase the Service User/Client's sense of purpose and hope, which are so important to Recovery. I believe that ultimately this will reduce the Revolving door syndrome. Don't just take my word for it, test it, research it for yourselves!

Chapter 5

Helpful qualities that make a good Coach

I am taking a look at at the helpful qualities of a good Coach at this point because when one is looking for a Coach one might think about what is helpful and what is not before purchasing their services. Some Coaches will give a free trial session a kind of "try before you buy".

In the book "An Introduction to Coaching for Health and Social Care". Page 26 written by Dilys Jones and Peter Murphy (Pavillion Publishing (Brighton) Ltd 2007) Lists:

Skills of a Coach

- recognition of strengths and development areas
- ability to empathise and to establish rapport
- pro-active approach
- ability to motivate Coachee
- ability to persist when the going gets tough
- ability to be flexible and to be patient
- ability to use a number of assessment tools or know where to refer people for them
- ability to challenge self limiting beliefs.

N.B. The word Coachee is another name for client or person being coached.

Attitudes

- respect for the Coachee and his or her beliefs
- interest in seeing the Coachee develop
- genuine desire to help Coachee
- empathy
- proactive approach
- values diversity

It would be useful to compare what the Client/Service User thinks important, to the academic lists above. Before I come to that I would like to tell you a little about Southwark Mind.

Southwark Mind is a mental health Charity in Southwark. Southwark

Mind is a Service User run organization and are largely a Campaigning organization. They fought for such things as to keep open the Emergency Clinic, which was eventually closed, but not before a safe place for Mental health Service Users in Accident and Emergency at Kings College Hospital was established.

Southwark Mind also has a SMUC these initials stand for Southwark Mind User Council where Service Users go onto the wards at the Maudsley Hospital and in drop ins to represent patients and other Service Users. SMUC also quizzes Health professionals about Services being provided by South London and Maudsley Foundation Trust (SLAM) in Southwark.

The other main project is the Kindred Minds, which is for Black Minority and Ethnic Service Users (BME). Initially I ran, on a voluntary basis, a trial Life Coaching project called Possibility (life) Coaching under the umbrella of Kindred Minds.

Brief out line of the Possibility(Life) Coaching project

I am a Professional Qualified Life Coach and Mental Health Service User. I suggested to Southwark Mind that Life Coaching could be helpful to other Service Users as part of the Recovery Model, after a funding meeting discussion with The Mental Health Foundation. I had previously used Life Coaching for Client/Service Users in 2004 with Greenwich Networks Trust Ltd, a BME Mental Health Charity, where it had been reasonably successful.

Anyway, to cut a long story short, after several meetings with Southwark Mind Executive, who are the trustees of Southwark Mind; who incidentally are all Service Users too, I managed to set up a trial Life Coaching project called Possibility (Life) Coaching. All I needed was a private room, advertising, a telephone, and stationery. Oh! and of course clients.

Between October 2009 – June 2010, I saw 7 clients who had between 6 to 12 sessions each. I want to introduce 3 of those clients. Their names are Kayin, Garry Ellison, and Mary Hernandez.

Introducing Kayin:

Kayin is a young Chinese woman, who has been using the Mental Health Services for 5 years, I first met her at the Launch of the Kindred Minds project back in 2007. She occasionally attended groups, one of which was a personal development group, facilitated by myself, called Building a Compelling Future. She made great strides forward during the 6 week Building a Compelling Future Course, which is done in a small group.

Kayin was the first client to use the Possibility (Life) Coaching project at Southwark Mind, she completed 11 out of the 12 sessions available. I am only speculating, but I guess she found endings difficult. I am going to list here what Kayin thinks are the helpful qualities that make a good Coach.

10 most helpful qualities that make a good Coach:

1. someone full of knowledge, plus has the skills to help motivate and empower me.
2. actively listens
3. supportive – focus on what is important to me and not their own agenda
4. friendly
5. honest, genuine
6. someone who does not impose their opinions on me
7. someone who helps me look at things I may need to challenge
8. shows empathy
9. able to comprehend what is being said and review sessions
10. someone who cares and shows they care

Introducing Garry Ellison

Garry is a man of West Indian heritage who has been using the Mental Health Services for approximately 5years. Garry had only previously attended one "Building a Compelling Future" personal development session before deciding it was not for him. However he seemed to like the Possibilities (Life) Coaching session, because it gave him privacy, as the sessions were done on a one to one basis.

Garry came to Life Coaching in 2009 and completed 9 sessions. Garry is friendly and has a raft of ideas and dreams. I asked Garry what he thought he saw as the 10 most helpful qualities in a good Coach?

10 most helpful qualities in a good Coach:

1. ability to actively listen
2. having some degree of identification with the person you are

      helping
3. having empathy
4. using empowering tools
5. having an unhurried demeanour
6. being (appropriately) available
7. being open minded
8. having respect for others' beliefs
9. rigorous honesty
10. being "driven" and purposeful to some degree

Next I want to introduce, Mary Hernandez, a South American woman who has used Mental Health Services for approximately 10 years. Mary had Possibility Life Coaching for 9 sessions.

Mary's 10 most helpful qualities of a good Coach are:

1. a good listener
2. non-aggressive
3. gentle
4. does not tell me what to do but gives some level of independence
5. somebody who cares about people and their well-being
6. able to talk to a person in a crisis
7. have strength
8. commitment
9. loyalty
10. a good memory

As you will observe, there are great similarities in the helpful qualities that Service User/clients look for in a good Coach. In fact they are not too far removed from the skills and attitudes mentioned in "an introduction to Coaching for Health and Social Care" listed by Dilys Jones and Peter Murphy, mentioned earlier. But perhaps a more specific comparison can be made with the qualities compiled by Professional Coach Sir John Whitmore, who wrote the book "Coaching for Performance" published by Brealey Publishing (London) 3rd Edition (2003). On page 41, Sir John Whitmore shares a list which one of his clients wrote:

Qualities of a Coach:

1. patient
2. detached
3. supportive

4. interested
5. good listener
6. perceptive
7. aware
8. self-aware
9. attentive
10. retentive

When I look at all the lists, I conclude there is less emphasis on technical ability, but more weight put on being human, and there is virtually no requirement of the Coach to solve their problems. There seems to be no extra requirements needed by the Service User/Client and the non Service User/Client. Both sets are more interested in the characteristics of the Coach ie whether they are interested, actively listens, honest, friendly, having respect for others' beliefs, non aggressive person, loyal etc.

Should we expect anything less when dealing with Coaches or Health Professionals, Social Workers etc.? For instance there have been about 3 General Practitioners in my life to date, yet I have never ever asked to see their qualifications or asked them where they trained. In fact I know nothing about them; now remember they literally hold my life in their hands. I actually know little or nothing about them, but what I do know is that they are all very good Doctors and I know this largely by the way they work with me as a patient. All I know is that they are good people whom
"*I can trust."*

I make this point because it is essential for the Coach to build a relationship with their client and I go further that it is imperative that Psychiatrists and other Health Professionals and Social Workers and the like do the same. Since technical skills yield better results if a good working relationship has been built with their clients.

The thread that runs through all the Service User/clients' and Sir John Whitmore's list is that the Coach must listen. Indeed there is also a common request from most Service Users that is echoed throughout the Mental Health Service, that Health Professionals listen to them.

FLOWERING SEEDS

(3 client/service users' outcomes after Life

Coaching).

Kayin:

As previously mentioned Kayin has had 11 Life Coaching sessions as part of the Possibility (Life) Coaching pilot at Southwark Mind, and has been using Mental Health Services for approximately 5 years.

Kayin is quite a well-mannered Woman but her drive to move forward is focused and determined. She is constantly searching for a better quality of life. Kayin came to me wanting to develop performance as a Trainer and she felt one of the ways she could improve this was learning to handle her intense anxiety levels, which limited other areas of her life.

After our ten sessions I asked Kayin to let me know whether she felt she gained any benefit from our Coaching sessions.

Kayin emailed the following:

The benefits from my Coaching sessions are:

I have tools to use to help for different situations e.g. relaxation or confidence techniques, when I am anxious, ways to increase my self-esteem and deal with negative thoughts. I have now the techniques to help myself, so that I can be more self reliant and move forward from being stuck.

The sessions were supportive, encouraging and helped guide me with what I wanted to work on e.g. I wanted help with increasing my confidence and motivation so that I could feel able to join an exercise class – sessions with Humphrey were really wonderful and helped me enormously to do this and now I am attending various dance and fitness classes because I have now got techniques to help me through the things I was finding enormously difficult.

I also have techniques I learnt during the Life Coaching sessions to help keep me attending the things I most want to do in my life and encouraging me if I ever feel de motivated or anxious………. An example of a massive thing I recently achieved that Humphrey's session helped me in was being able to attend a Conference as a guest speaker to an audience of over 50 people.

Email sent 13th November 2009 approximately 2 months after her last Coaching Session.

Thought Bubbles

Notice I have not given you, the reader, any case history or details of her diagnosis. This is because I deliberately did not ask her. What I am doing with Coaching is looking at where my client wants to go; not necessarily where they have been. As far as diagnosis is concerned I have no medical knowledge and I really do not understand what it means.

The above concept of not asking about diagnosis or requesting case histories happens all the time in drop-in centres where we take people first as people. I guess some of my readers may be saying working with someone in a one to one session is a whole different kettle of fish to working in a busy drop -in. My answer to that, I have in the past set up a Counselling Service in a National Schizophrenia Fellowship drop-in service in Milton Keynes where Service Users only told us what they felt was relevant. This was nearer to the Person Centred model.

Kayin writes: **"I have now techniques to help so that I can be more self-reliant."** Its the words *I can be more self-reliant* that I want you to focus on. This is what makes the difference and can be a useful aid to the Recovery Model. What most Service Users often want is a greater level of independence. The problem with some of the Mental Health services is that you have to keep going back to a Health Professional. For example in 1981 after becoming Mentally ill I was told to take Pimozide now almost 30 years later I am taking 5 different types of medication and most of that time I have had to see a Psychiatrist. It has through the years made me dependent, I sometimes wonder if in the long term it would have been cheaper to have talking therapies.

Kayin also writes: **"an example of a massive thing I achieved recently that Humphrey's session helped me with was being able to attend a conference as a guest speaker to an audience of over 50 people"**.

Wherever possible I try to encourage the client to have a tangible goal, so that they too can see or otherwise recognize the difference. So that they can say "I did this!" That way it is easier for the client and the Coach to see what is working and what is not working. To this end it is advisable for the Coach to encourage the client to choose a specific goal to work towards. It should be noted that really all I did was help her build her self-esteem using Life Coaching as a vehicle. Incidentally, the Conference that Kayin spoke at was at the Lord Mayor of London's residence, City Hall near Tower Bridge.

SNAP SHOT QUESTIONNAIRE FOR LIFE COACHING.

DATE 1st September 2010

Note: details of the client's Mental health diagnosis is not required by the Life Coach, because of confidentiality and because it is important for the Life Coach to be unfettered by diagnosis and the stigma that comes with it. Since the Life Coach is unlikely to be trained in Medical matters such disclosure is unlikely to be helpful. What matters is that the client wants to move on in their life.

Questionnaire:

Name: *Kayin*

1) What was your main goal?

To reduce my anxieties and to commit to the things I want to do (e.g. martial arts) despite feelings of anxiety.

2) When did you start Life Coaching with Humphrey?

Last year

3) How long have you had Life Coaching for?

10 weeks

4) Have you noticed any differences or changes since having Life Coaching, if so list examples:

Yes, I've noticed that I am using some of those techniques, still that I have learnt e.g. finger and thumb for confidence, imagining events going the best they can (visualizing them in a positive light.) to reduce anxieties. They have been really helpful.

5) If you have noticed any differences or changes after having Life Coaching. How long ago did you desire to make those changes? If any?

I have wanted to make changes about my anxieties all my life. After Life Coaching I made changes that helped me cope with anxieties and it surprisingly opened many doors for me in a positive way! I started getting opportunities I couldn't before even dream of.

6) Do you feel you have more or less options after Life Coaching? List examples:

Definitely more options – I've gained so many positive tips out of the Coaching.

I've learnt some very quick practical tips on how to change my state (e.g. from anxiety/fear to more confident . The quotes Humphrey gave me were inspiring.

7) Would you say your quality of life has:
   a) Improved   b) Stayed the same   c) Got worse
Please tick as appropriate.

Describe briefly the quality of your life today after Coaching.

Improved, when using the techniques learnt from Coaching it has helped me to go for things – set a goal list and achieve a lot of them. So I've been able to commit to things much better.

8) How would you describe your level of self esteem after Coaching?
   a) Poor   b) OK   c) Very good   d) Indifferent

Very good. When I use the Coaching materials it helps me to achieve my goals, take action and see things/myself more positively.

9) If Life Coaching has made a difference to your self-esteem state how:

It's helped me realize that if I just push through the fear I amaze myself with what I can achieve and that gives me a sense of being a better person, being useful and able to do good things, and capable of doing a lot of things.

10) Have other people in your life noticed any differences? Since your Life Coaching sessions?

Yes, people have seen my confidence grow because as I use my techniques to achieve my goals and push through my fears. My confidence grows and people can see and sense it. People sense the Power and the confidence that shines through me. People see that I have grown and comment on the positive change.

11) Did you achieve your main goal?
    (Yes)   (Shift towards it)   (No)

Yes, and also I have kept myself shifting towards it because it is constant and Never ending improvement. I need to keep working on my anxieties/fears if I stop I will go backwards and things will get worse for me

12) Have you got any dreams or goals you wish to achieve?

I want to start organizing my own courses where I go out and promote myself. Liaise with potential participants or clients and run courses myself. I have recently filled in an application form to go on a course. I was fearful of filling the application form and many times I did not believe I was capable of doing it. But I tried it and did my best. I was offered an interview for the selection process where I was given feed back that my application was very very strong and brilliant. (I was selected to go on a course and completed it).

I also have a goal to help others through voluntary work and I have applied for the position to help at a Care Home for Mental Health Service Users. I have got an interview and opportunity to meet staff and clients next week. (I got through the tough interview and started voluntary work there supporting residents.

I want to own a business and be wealthy so that I can help a huge amount of people- using my money as a vehicle to reach out to many more.

I want a flexible life style, work when I want to. I want to settle down with one person, have a family together, be happy and always be developing in a positive way.

    13)   What was the greatest insight you gained through Life Coaching?

The quotes, the visualization, seeing things in a positive light and imagining things going well. The best thing is feeling confident and good; and that I am able to cope.

    14)   What in your Life Coaching sessions made the greatest impact on you?

It's got to be the visualization technique of seeing things going in the best way they can and imagining the confidence. I feel happiness from it, and imagining that I already completed what I want to achieve it and imagining the best possible outcome. This is one of the greatest ways that helped me break through intense anxieties that held me back for most of my life.

The results have been fantastic when I've used this technique e.g. when I was really fearful about a training course I was going to deliver, I felt physically sick, I did the visualizations of the best possible way it could go. I delivered the course so confidently and even better than I could have ever imagined! This has happened on a few occasions and also different situations e.g. speaking up in class which I almost never do.

    15)   The Life Coach sometime gives you tools to use when appropriate e.g. relaxation techniques. What tool, if any, has been helpful?

Visualization, finger and thumb for confidence. Sedona Method for deleting negative thoughts.

QUESTIONS ABOUT YOUR LIFE COACH:

    16)   How did you find the Coach?
           a) Helpful   b) OK   c) Unhelpful.

Very helpful. He has a lot of fantastic knowledge. Humphrey is a fantastic inspiring Life Coach – he aimed to put me first and what I wanted to work on in each session. He would also prepare things for the next session that would fit in with what I wanted to achieve.

    17)   a) What worked well?
           b) What did not work so well?

a) The way Humphrey and I worked well together. I liked his style and method of working – the quotes, practical techniques, the language used, the info given, the examples used were all very inspiring, empowering, helpful and I can keep using these techniques myself.

b) There was nothing that did not work well.

    18)   Would you have Life Coaching again if you needed it?

Yes, definitely – Life Coaching helped in so many areas of my life but because I am ambitious and would like to move onto other things. I would like help in other areas too.

Finally, do you feel that Life Coaching has improved your chances of recovery from Mental ill Health?

Yes I feel Life Coaching has improved my chances of recovery. I know to maintain/improve my recovery I will have to keep going back to my materials I have learnt from Coaching and apply them.

Thought Bubbles

Kayin's last session was the 9th September 2009 and she gave me the feedback about the Coaching on the 13th November 2009 approximately 2 months after the last Coaching session. Followed by a Snapshot questionnaire on the 1st September 2010 just under a year after Kayin's last Coaching session.

Kayin is still using the tools/techniques independently, in the Snapshot questionnaire she places even greater emphasis on the tools/techniques than being Coached. To me this signals greater growth of independence, the presence of the Coach is no longer required and is seen as less relevant to the process. If the client has to keep coming back or feels unable to function without the Coach I believe this reduces the effectiveness of Coaching. Otherwise what happens when the Coach is no longer able to be there?

Under question 11 of the Snapshot questionnaire is the realisation from Kayin that using the tools is an on-going process "constant and never ending improvement." The difference being now a choice whether or not to use the tools, but more importantly she has her independence.

Under question 12 of the Snapshot questionnaire she lists some of the dreams and goals she wishes to achieve from running her own Training courses to getting married and settling down. This highlights the presence of hope in Kayin's life. Hope being an important cornes tone on which to build recovery. Kayin herself says **"I feel Life Coaching has improved my chances of recovery."**

Again she says she will refer back to the material gained during the Coaching session. In a Coaching session I would normally give the Client/Service User a clipboard with some paper and a pen where they can make notes of what they think is important. If they prefer they can draw instead as their Coach I will also have a clip board etc. for making notes which I will give to them once all the Coaching session are finished. Whereas the Client/Service User can take the notes they make away with them after each individual session.

As an aside, Kayin continues to grow. I saw her deliver a talk to approximately 80 Student Social Workers at the London South Bank University in 2010.

Garry Ellison

As aforesaid, Garry is a man of West Indian heritage who has used the Mental Health Services for 5 years . Gary had 9 Life Coaching sessions, the last one ending on the 6th December 2009. The following account was submitted by Garry about 2 months after his last session.

Garry writes:

Approximately a year ago, after feeling I was at a loose end I began to embark on researching ways to positively go forward with my life.

I had been on ESA (Employment Support Allowance), as I had to stop work a year before, and I wanted to explore a possible change of career as well as a more defined purpose in life. It was around this time I met Humphrey Greaves, who delivered Life Coaching courses to Mental Health Service Users. I felt such a course could be beneficial in helping to find direction.

The course was a 12 week one and it looked at practical ways of setting personal goals. This practical approach of setting personal goals was very useful as we recorded progress from week to week. I was also given examples of how other (famous) people came to realise their dreams.

The course has helped me to sharpen my focus on the priorities of my purpose. I have now progressed in the direction I feel I was supposed to.

Things I am doing now:

Counselling Course,
Working on the Involvement register,
Service User Committee work,
Patient experience data intelligence centred work with South side partnership.

Thought Bubbles

Garry has made some important points one of which was that he was given practical tools to use e.g. The personal goal setting tools. the problem with some interventions used in Mental health is that things are done to you rather than working with you. Any consultation seems to revolve around finance, i.e. can the Health system afford it, or else the intervention is so complicated you need a PHD to understand it.

Life Coaching, on the other hand, tries to be as open as possible. No smoking mirrors. In fact I would go further if the Client/Service User does not understand how to use the tool practically, then they are probably not going to use it. It is not how complicated a tool or intervention is, it is whether it works and whether it can used by the Client/Service User.

Garry mentions my examples of famous people and their struggle to succeed. I call this the Myth of the over night success, to know that famous people went through their trials too helps put into perspective bold media claims that sometimes set unrealistic expectations on others. This can lower self esteem.

Snap shot questionnaire for Life Coaching

Date 10th September 2010

Note: Details of the client's Mental health diagnosis is not required by the Life Coach because of confidentiality and because it is important for Life Coach to be unfettered by diagnosis and stigma that comes with it. Since the Life Coach is unlikely to be trained in Medical matters such disclosure is likely to be unhelpful. What matters is that the client wishes to move on in their Life.

Questionnaire

Name: *Garry Ellison*

1) What was your main goal?

To help black people in Mental Health Services, who seem to be experiencing prolonged periods of stagnation and decline, recover and/or achieve a reasonably good quality of life via a network of peers with lived experience helping each other.

2) When did you start Life Coaching with Humphrey?

About a year ago.

3) How long did you have Life Coaching for?

10 weeks.

4) Have you noticed any differences or changes since having Life Coaching? If so list examples:

1) More confidence that my ideas can work
2) Better at feasibility assessment
3) I am more patient and methodical
4)   Decision making seems to have improved

5) If you have noticed any differences or changes after having Life Coaching. How long ago did you desire to make those changes? If any?

Quite a few years.

6) Do you feel you have more or less options after Life Coaching? List examples:

1) My original ideas can and have been expanded
2) I have decided on some areas of study to enhance my usefulness to others
3)   I have found more resources available to me

7) Would you say your quality of life has:
    a) Improved   b) Stayed the same   c) Got worse

a) Improved

My overall quality of Life has improved as I have now expanded, hypothetically speaking, my field of vision and all areas of my life have been positively enhanced with this new sight.

8)   How would you describe your level of self esteem after Life Coaching?
    a) Poor   b) OK   c) Very good   d) Indifferent

Very good

9) If Life Coaching has made a difference to your self esteem state how:

My overall quality of life has improved as I have now expanded, hypothetically speaking, my field of vision and all areas of my life have been positively enhanced with this new sight.

10) Have other people in your life noticed any differences? Since your Life Coaching sessions?

Absolutely.

11) Did you achieve your main goal?
(Yes)   (a shift towards)   (No)
Please tick as appropriate

Yes

12) Have you got any dreams or goals you wish to achieve?

To help black people in Mental Health Services, who seem to be experiencing prolonged periods of stagnation and decline, recover and/or achieve a reasonably good quality of life via a network of peers with a lived experience helping each other.

13) What is the greatest insight you gained through Life Coaching?

Different perspectives.

14) What in your life Coaching sessions made the greatest impact on you?

Examples of success in others.

15) The Life Coach sometimes gives you tools to use when appropriate e.g. relaxation techniques.

Relaxation techniques and re assessment skills

Questions about your Coach:

16) How did you find your Life Coach?

    a) Helpful   b) OK   c) Unhelpful

a) Helpful

17)   a) What worked well?

Looking at different ways to tackle the same problem

    b) What did not work well?

N/A

18) Would you have Life Coaching again if you needed it?

Yes

Finally, do you feel that Life Coaching has improved your chances of recovery from Mental ill health?

Yes

Thought Bubbles

Garry states in question (4) that he has *more confidence that my ideas will work* which is balanced by what he calls being *better at feasibility assessment.* This growth in confidence and his ability to see what is workable is a great step forward.

As part of the Coaching experience clients are asked to look at what I call their current reality as well as their current resources. This should not be used as an excuse to be condescending but to help the Client/Service User work out for themselves what will work and what will not.

Garry has also found he has been more patient and that his decision making has improved. The good thing is that Garry has not sat down each week and waited for me to give a designer fit answer to his questions he has been encouraged to be proactive. For instance Garry decided to take a Counselling course because he wanted to understand Boundaries.

I explained that I was not the fountain of all knowledge, that is I did not have all the answers. That I was part of the jigsaw that may help to facilitate him in finding what he was looking for.

Garry took control. Sometimes this is done just by suggesting they look something up on the computer, other times may be in more subtle ways.

Garry also stated in question 9) that *my overall quality of life has improved.* I believe he achieved this by taking greater control of his life thus growing in belief in himself.

One of the things which Gary felt worked well was *looking at different ways to tackle the same problem.* We as a Society seem to get so fussed about doing some things a certain way we impose them rather than explain them. Anyway, often there is somewhere in the world where someone is doing, safely, exactly what we say should not be done e.g. mountaineers, divers who swim with Sharks; I would not recommend it; but it's being done. So it is with more everyday things. encouraging each other to look at our options is just so liberating.

Mary Hernandez

Mary Hernandez is a South American woman who has been using the Mental Health Services for 10 years. Mary started Life Coaching with me on the 14th October 2009 on the Possibility (Life) Coaching pilot scheme at Southwark Mind. Mary Hernandez had 9 Coaching sessions with the Possibility (Life) Coaching pilot scheme.

Mary Hernandez writes:

The course of Life Coaching with Humphrey has helped me in many ways. When I started I was feeling lethargic, tired, depressed and I did not see a way out of my situation. On top of that the Government was putting lots of pressure on me to get back to work, I felt I was in a closed road.

The most important thing is he listened to me and at the same time did not let me dwell on my problems, just concentrated on looking for solutions. One problem was resolved at a time. Suddenly, I felt lighter and more positive. Around me people feel the change in me, They are trying to help too.

I am less depressed and I feel that whatever life throws at me I will deal with it, resolving one thing at a time. I am looking forward to the rest of the sessions to see how I am doing. I have found that Life Coaching is as helpful as other therapies I have done, it did push me forward.

Thought Bubbles

Mary highlights that she felt listened to and appreciated, that she was not left to dwell on her problems. Life Coaching is proactive, an important part of G.R.O.W. Model Coaching is looking at other options. Sometimes they involve looking at different approaches. Sometimes it is just about being there.

Where possible I encouraged Mary to get into action rather than worry about what might happen, rather than encourage her to delve too deeply into problems. I leave that to other therapists: what my Coaching is about is dealing with the here and now. As the saying goes: yesterday is a cancelled cheque, tomorrow is a promissory note.

I like to point out the independence factor again, Mary says:

I am less depressed and I feel that whatever life throws at me I will deal with it.

Mary now feels she is in control she feels she can now deal with it. She does not necessarily have to come back to the Coach, she can handle it.

Important to note that Mary says *Coaching is as helpful as other therapies I have done.* As a Coach I hope it is at least as Mary says, because I am definitely not saying that Life Coaching should replace Psychiatry or any other medicine or even Counselling or therapy. I would say that Life Coaching is there, in this context, to help Service Users have a smooth transition back into the community and to encourage them in their personal growth. Mary says, *it did push me forward.*

In fact after the sessions with the Possibility (Life) Coaching sessions came to an end. Mary approached me and asked if she could become a client of my Coaching Practice called Humphrey Greaves Coaching Practice which I run privately. She is now a client of mine working on new goals.

Snap shot questionnaire for Life Coaching.

Date 6th August 2010

Note Details of the client's Mental Health diagnosis is not required by the Life Coach because of confidentiality and because it is important for the Life Coach to be unfettered by diagnosis and the stigma that comes with it. Since the Life Coach is unlikely to be trained in medical matters such disclosure is likely to be unhelpful. What matters is that the client wishes to move on in their life.

Questionnaire:

Name: *Mary Hernandez*

1) What was your main goal?

I was being pressured to go back to work, the Coach had already done it. Money issues, help with money issues, going back to school, building self-esteem, confidence.

2) When did you start Life Coaching with Humphrey?

End of October 2009

3) How long have you had Life Coaching for?

10 sessions and a further 8 months privately.

4) Have you noticed any differences or changes since having Life Coaching? If so list examples:

My self esteem is much better, I feel good about myself, and I feel quite proud of myself. I don't feel ashamed any more. Now I feel more fore fulfilled and motivated.

5) If you have noticed any differences or changes after having Life Coaching. How long ago did you desire to make those changes? If any?

30 years.

6) Do you feel you have more options after Life Coaching? List examples:

a) I want to make an Art Studio
b) I have a few business ideas
c) I want to visit the countryside.

7) Would you say your quality of Life has:
   a) Improved   b) Stayed the same   c) Got worse

a) Improved

Describe briefly the quality of your life today after Coaching?

More peace of mind - before I had a serious problem with my daughter's school but I am now feeling more positive.

8) How would you describe your level of self esteem after Life Coaching?
   a) Poor   b) OK   c) Very good   d) Indifferent

c)   Very good

9) If Life Coaching has made a difference to your self-esteem state how?

Already answered

10) Have other people in your life noticed any differences? Since your Life Coaching sessions?

I want the confidence to go and learn computers.

11) Did you achieve your main goal?
(Yes)   (A shift towards)   (No)

A shift towards

12) Have you got any dreams or goals you wish to achieve?

Fashion design, selling through auctions, my own studies, more financial freedom.

13) What was the greatest insight you gained through Life Coaching?

Learning about me and not beating myself up any more.

14) What in your Life Coaching sessions made the greatest impact on you?

Being able to talk in confidence and the way the Coach calms me down in a crisis.

15) The Life Coach sometimes gives you tools to use when appropriate e.g. relaxation techniques. What tools if any have been helpful?

Index card with Sedona Method, being told I am a valuable person, I am no longer a doormat.

Questions about your Life Coach:

16) How helpful did you find your Life Coach?
a) Helpful   b) OK   c) Unhelpful

a) Helpful

17) a) What worked well?

When my life is in a crisis and everything becomes huge the Coach takes a specific thing one at a time and it becomes more manageable.

b) What did not work well?

It was OK.

18) Would you have Life Coaching again if you needed it?

Yes

Finally, do you feel that Life Coaching has improved your chances of recovery from Mental ill Health?

Yes, it has given me the structure that I need to recover to work on myself bit by bit. I am not blocked or stuck.

Thought Bubbles

Mary Hernandez is a determined and thoughtful Woman and under question 4 of the Snapshot questionnaire she describes her Self-Esteem as feeling much better, feeling good about herself. This is such an important stage to dwell in on the road to Recovery. I believe once a person has good self-esteem almost anything is possible. Not only that Mary has written down a few dreams she wishes to achieve i.e. Making an art Studio, she has a few business ideas.

Often when one is experiencing Mental ill Health our self-esteem is low and our hopes and dreams have reached rock bottom. It is important to give hope to the Service User, especially if she or he is going to play a full part in Society. By encouraging the Service User to be independent where possible, it may also help to set them free.

Signposting is sometimes a good way of encouraging us to look for ourselves. For instance Mary Hernandez has done various courses with different organizations to help her progress, not just Coaching. Coaching has been one of her tools, but Coaching is not about doing for a person or even doing it with a person necessarily, but encouraging the person to take charge and do it for themselves.

Mary has wanted to make some of the changes she has made in her life with Life Coaching for over 30 years, see question 5 of the Snapshot questionnaire. I believe had the Mental Services taken into account her cultural needs and taken the time to get alongside her, her life may have taken a more positive path. Mary has been with the Mental Health Services for approximately 10years now.

The Coaching relationship - a fundamental of Coaching

The Coaching relationship which is how a Coach and client work together is a fundamental requirement of Coaching. The relationship has similarities to that between a Counsellor and their client. For Counsellors who practice Person-Centred Counselling their relationship with their Client is the vital ingredient, so the relationship between Coach and client is likewise a vital ingredient for Coaching. Without the Coaching relationship no Coaching takes place. It is for this reason that I only work with people who want to be Coached; so in terms of working with Client/Service User, I will only work with them if I have their consent. I will not knowingly be Coaching them at the behest of a Doctor or Psychiatrist or Social Worker or Carer, no! I require my Coaching clients to willingly Consent, put bluntly they have got to want to be Coached.

As a Coach I feel it is up to me to try and create a safe space for the client to come and work. One of the ways of doing this is to create clear boundaries and knowing the Coaches' Confidentiality Policy lets the client know where they stand. As a Coach I convey my Confidentiality Policy before I start Coaching work with them. I believe the Coach should be up front about the policy so that it gives the client the chance to decide what they will and will not tell you. I believe they too should have the choice what they disclose. As a Coach I really only need to know what they think is relevant to the Coaching process, I work in the Here and Now, I am neither a retrospective Guru nor a Fortune-teller. My basic Confidentiality Policy is:

"Everything is Confidential unless you are likely to harm yourself or others, or if I am legally required to disclose, or if you give your consent to disclosure."

Having a particular time and place to meet can also help the client feel safe, this might be a particular room but not always. My sessions usually last about 45 minutes to an hour and generally happen about once a week for each client. I generally do about 6 sessions per client with an upper limit of 12 sessions.

The Coach should be non critical and non judgemental.

It is not for the Coach to look down on, patronize or criticize their clients but to show respect. Basically if a Coach is unable to show respect to their client, maybe the Coach should not be working with that client. Coaching is a Human to Human experience, requiring that the individuals treat each other as equals and with respect. Irrespective of their past whether or not you knew them in the past or not, it is the Coaches job to work with the Here and Now. If the Coach cannot work with their prospective client for any reason, then they should tell them and make the necessary referral if required.

Trust

This comes with openness and respect this is true of Coaching as it is when people meet in Society. We often try to discern how trustworthy a person is before we start talking to them. The more trustworthy we perceive that person to be the higher the upgrade of personal information is likely to be. As a Coach your trustworthiness rating with your client needs to be right up there.

The business world knows its potential customers need to trust the Company and the product it wants to sell by directly tapping into our "Can I trust this" detector, by posting known Celebrities seemingly endorsing the product. For instance the Model Kate Moss and Top shop, The Formula one Racing Driver Lewis Hamilton a former World Champion and Santander Bank. Sometimes Celebrities will impliedly endorse products by appearing in a photograph, using them on our television screens right before our very eyes or by verbal communication. Leaving the customer feeling the product must be good because the chosen Celebrity uses it.

The business Marketing people normally choose someone who is well known and whom the public are likely to trust. Should the person they choose loose the public's trust or be perceived to have lost their trust, then it is likely they will be dropped from the Marketing Campaign. It is that brutal. So too, Clients can drop the Coach or put up barriers preventing the Coaching relationship developing.

The Coaching relationship is a fundamental of Coaching, since effective Coaching cannot take place easily without it. There is no reason why any one should share parts with another if they can not trust them, even if that other person wears a badge saying Doctor, Psychiatrist, Nurse or Social Worker. Who are they anyway? Just another Human being with a badge. Building the relationship is essential, it can be the difference that makes the difference!

In Coaching the Client/Service User will often lead you to where they want to take you, it is called following the client's interest.

Upstarts are makers of future history.

A little History. I started practising Neuro Linguistic Programming (NLP) having become a Practitioner in 2000. One of the clients who came to me was a lady called Tia we seemed to work well together but something was missing. The NLP sessions were O,K, and we ended the sessions via mutual consent.

Anyway I pondered the sessions, there did not seem to be anything wrong with NLP, I concluded that there was something about me that was wrong. Later I came across Life Coaching, where I learned about developing the Coaching relationship between Coach and client. This proved to be the difference that made the difference.

In my first Coaching session with Tia at Greenwich Networks Trust which was a Mental Health Charity. I asked her if she could do, be or have anything what would that be? Instantly she said she would like to sing; note I did not teach her to sing, she could already do that. Besides my neighbours do not take too kindly to my singing, so I thought I would refrain from inflicting it on the general population. I simply encouraged her to follow her own yellow brick road. Tia followed her dream she sang at a Conference before the Lord Mayor of Greenwich and Baroness Howes of St Davids, she has also sung publicly at Southwark Minds "Get to me Know Me First" Conference at the Mayor of London's residence City Hall near Tower Bridge. Bearing in mind, before arranging for Tia to sing before the Lord Mayor of Greenwich and Baroness Howells of St David's. I had never heard Tia sing live before; but such was the Coaching relationship; we trusted each other thus helping to build her self esteem and self belief. To make history you have to be an upstart, Tia was making her own personal history.

Basically Tia had to feel she trusted me, she had to feel I would be there whatever the outcome, she had to trust me with her precious dream of singing. The quickest way to build trust is to listen and be non-judgemental; it is refreshing to be listened to, especially if the listener shows empathy. If the Client/Service User is not listened to, the Coaching relationship becomes stunted and unable to grow. Coaching time should mean quality time.

Chapter 6

Recovery or Bust

There are possibly as many Recovery Models as there are people who have experienced Mental ill health. Now is that an outlandish statement? Well it is often felt that Recovery is an individual journey for each Service User and/or each Patient. For instance, one Service User who is suffering from anxiety may decide that Recovery for them is just to get to the front door, whilst another may decide to walk to work is Recovery for them. It is up to the Service User to set the standard. Some might say that Recovery is as individual as the grains of sand, and quite right too.

The individuality of Recovery often frightens the Economists and such like planners and strategists because its a notion that appears to relinquish their control. For me much of Mental Health medicine is about restraint and control. I will acknowledge that there are times when the Service User wants to give up control, but Recovery should be about helping the Service User regain control not taking the Service User over. If the Service User is to regain his or her independence he or she must take the helm.

I know it may seem ridiculous to some that the patient or Service User should decide when they have recovered and may seem an alien concept to the Medical Profession etc. The Medical Profession should not be alarmed by this. In general medicine, do not Health Professionals seek the opinion of the patient? Do they not ask "and how are you feeling? Do you feel well enough to go home? There at least the patient's experience is acknowledged, this is not always so with Mental Health. I have been using Mental health services for 30 years and cannot remember being asked if I was feeling any better. I do not know if you can recall the big containers which were taken off the Docks they used to call the procedure "roll on, roll off. Sometimes it feels like, we are just cargo.

HUMAN TO HUMAN

I slipped down a deep dark tunnel and all I could think was: when they find me, will they remember I am human?

Cuts and tightening of the belt endanger the Recovery Model as services clamber to reduce expenditure to balance the books. I believe that taking time to encourage Recovery will save tears later.

So in line with that, why not ask each service user or patient what Recovery means to them from the outset, instead of waiting to the end or discharge? At least all parties would know what they are working towards. Ask what Recovery looks like, sounds like and feels like for them? The more descriptive they are the better the picture you have of how they will know when they have Recovered. In short one could ask how will they know they have Recovered? You will in effect have the blue print of their Recovery or a goal they want to work towards.

By simply following the Grow Model, like the Life Coach, i.e. G = Goal, R = reality and resources, O = Options, W = Willingness to act. As far as the"R" is concerned I add the words current reality and current resources, it helps to see things in a practical light.

Sometimes taking the client/Service User through this can be an eye opener for both Service User and professionals. I generally ask my Client/Service Users to walk me through their current reality and ask them what their current resources are. Despite media hype, many Service Users are highly skilled and have a tapestry of life experiences.

Recovery has become the buzz word of mental health and rightly so, in my opinion, for what is the point of going to any sort of hospital if you do not recover? I am not talking about Hospices here or the like, I am talking about hospitals and in particular Mental Health hospitals. The Service user or patient can not say twist I will have another card of life, it is not a like a game of Pontoon. Yet you would not think after all these years of treating people for mental ill health that Recovery would still be an alien concept. In his book called "Recovery - an alien concept" published by P&P Publishing Press Wormit Fife (2004) Page 19, Ron Coleman writes:

The belief in Recovery from serious mental illness is almost non-existent in western Psychiatry, in its place we have adopted a concept of maintenance and social control for those we deem to be mentally ill. Does this mean that recovery is not possible for those classed as mentally ill? Or is it merely that we have put too much effort in to the present system in order to ensure a recovery process that would work? Or have we lost the knowledge and the skills that are required to work with people in a way that will enable Recovery.

Ron Coleman is a Service User, Author and Speaker. Ron Coleman was in the Psychiatric system for 13 years, diagnosed with

Schizophrenia; Ron Coleman used the Hearing Voices Network to aid his Recovery. Hearing Voices was founded by Marius Romme and Sandra Escher. (The Hearing Voices Network website is www.hearing-voices network.org.)

It seems that attitudes and practices in Mental health history have had a very polarised outlook, cure or suspend life's journey until we can find another cure. By suspending life's journey I mean they give medication that effectively keeps the Service User in Mothballs to the extent that the Service User is no longer able to function in society. This could take the form of them being asleep all the time, and/or being so obese they can hardly move for example. Sometimes the Service User's quality of life is significantly reduced by medication side effects.

From the late 1990's onwards Professionals were becoming aware of other steps along the continuum, for instance various Recovery Models started to surface e.g. the Tidal Model, Recovery Star Approach (Mental Health Providers' Forum 2009), Perkins and Repper (Social Inclusion and Recovery. A Model for Mental Health Practice 2006). Further, the English Government in 2001 adopted the Recovery Approach as an Official strategy (Department of Health 2001). Today the Current Government seems to be focused on just returning Service Users back to work without, I might add, the help of meaningful transition.

Very often in this world we want the "One cap fits all" solution but what about the individual? I have done it too! For instance I once tried to start a business. There I was in Brixton trying to get members of the General Public to buy things from my catalogues giving my specially learned spiel. A man watched me, listened, then said: "how is that going to help me?" There was silence and he walked away. I did not know the answer, mainly because I never asked anything like, "what are you looking for?" Or ask him about his individual needs. All I did was reel off my spiel from a memorised crib card. I was just focused on obtaining large amounts of money which, surprise, surprise, never came. Personally, I think the rules are similar with Governments, who forget the people; and focus solely on making money. It will end in disaster in the long term. Whilst empowering the Service User, getting to know them first, working with them, will I suggest, bring just rewards, it's what might be called a win win outcome.

The Customer is always right or should I say the Service User

is always right?

Interesting concept, sometimes in sleepy Hospital Board room meetings the Service User is referred to as the customer. I prefer, as I said, to be called the client as it makes me feel more in control. But whatever your preference, customer does give an element of control. The 1920's shop keeper's adage was: "the customers always right!" This might make Service providers listen to Service Users, since Service Users may in reality become the paying customers. If the Service User customers should feel that Service providers, Health Professionals, Social Workers etc. are not delivering on aiding their Recovery they may refuse to pay them. That may become a reality with the advent of "individual budgets", it may well change the shape of Mental health care, if it is extended.

Us Service Users also have to change our mindset, instead of being passive receivers of care we need to claim our mantle and take charge of our lives. I am not talking in the physical sense when I talk of passive receivers or even necessarily in the political sense, I am simply talking in the sense of our outlook, our mindset etc.

All I know is, often it's just the patient or Service User in the Consulting room with the Psychiatrist or Community Psychiatric Nurse, the world watches with unseeing eyes; technically they could say anything, if you have not got the self-esteem and self-belief to ask for help, then you may never get that Advocate. I know Service Users are normally entitled to an advocate if you are sectioned, but that misses the point. They have got to have enough self-worth or self-esteem to instruct their Advocate, self-esteem is not always a given, when one is depressed for instance. It can be extremely difficult, to say the least, just to ask for the simplest things sometimes. But however difficult, at the end of the day we Service Users need to take charge of our own lives.

Keynote Speech:

Don't let life catch you waiting for an alibi.

No matter how carefully crafted your alibi
No matter how well rehearsed
No matter the skill of your Lawyer
No matter the pleading

You either make the most of life or you don't

So don't let life catch you waiting for an alibi
Take charge of life, live it now!

I realise there are different degrees of health and I acknowledge that, but taking charge of our own lives can be liberating, it can be a catalyst for a better future. When I am depressed, I sometimes feel suicidal, but note my suicidal feelings are often coupled with feelings of doom, lack of control over my life etc. However, when I take responsibility for my life, I am able to challenge the negative thoughts. I am then often able to begin to turn things around. I feel hopeful, and in time regain my zest and passion for life.

I am suggesting here that Life Coaching can be used as a tool of Recovery but the Service User/Client must set their own goals, not the Health Professionals.

Keynote Speech:

Doing your own Goal thing!

Never mind the shoulds, should nots, must haves . What about me? What about my goals?

We go through life being told what we must do, be, or have. You do not believe me? Watch any television program or read the newspaper or listen to the radio or better still see how things are presented to us and sold in shops i.e. " buy now while stocks last" tells us we must buy now as it could be our last opportunity.

Or cast your mind back to your School days, must get straight A's must get a good job, must get a fast car, must get a partner, must get a big house, must have 2.2 children, must look good in clothes, must have the perfect body and so on.

The trouble with all this is that they are often other people's goals. Like parents or Teachers, employers, the media, Psychiatrists etc. Think for a moment how many people have actually asked you what you really wanted and listened to what you had to say? Without telling you what you should want? Often the people who tell us what we ought to have as a goal know very little about us personally as individuals. All society knows is what it wants. So it is up to you as individuals to take charge of your life and set your own goals.

WHO ELSE CAN?

POTENTIAL

Dictionary definition of potential is: possible but not actual (From Collins soft back English Dictionary 1992 published by Harper Collins)

In the Dictionary of Counselling by Colin Feltham and Windy Dryden published by Whurr Publishers (1993). Potential is defined as the power to become. Potential can mean anything which is not, and therefore may yet be.

Whilst in the book called "the NLP Coach: a comprehensive guide to personal success and well being & professional success" by Ian McDermott and Wendy Jago published by Piatkus (2004). States: Potential isn't a fixed quantity. The word is derived from the Latin potentia, meaning power or ability – itself derived from the verb " to be able". Potential then is the capacity to learn and develop which is inherent in everyone.

Potential is a word that is not often used in relation to Mental health; very often, Health professionals see us Service Users in terms of dysfunction and needing to be fixed. Instead of what we might become. The Mental health professional thinks in terms of risk and potential risk.

Somewhere along the line, and I suggest it is especially required in the Recovery stage, we, the Service User, need to be given hope. One way of doing this is to look at our potential and how we can make a valuable contribution to Society. When I talk about potential I mean it is an individual thing, and the Service User should choose whether or not they wish to use that potential and how they use it. We do not need a Government Directive on how or whether we should use our potential, the choice should be ours!

Potential should be associated with growth instead of the Medical Profession, Social Workers and the like just looking to see how they can fix us. It might give a new angle on any treatment we are receiving. Looking from the view of potential growth might evoke a sense of hope in the Service User. A change of mindset by all concerned could improve the chances of recovery.

I mentioned some celebrities earlier, who have experienced Mental ill health and it's great that they are still doing what they are doing, but what about looking at the potential of those of us who are not so famous? I am not necessarily talking about stardom, what about a little praise, a little encouragement goes a long way, you do not have to be an Impresario to give it. From a little encouragement great confidence can grow, who knows what will happen?

Everyone wants to make a difference.

It is not so popular these days to send out scouts seeking potential and to develop that potential helping it to grow. We want the ready-made ideal employee, the big celebrity head liner, the multimillion pound footballer, the millionaire businessman, right down to our ready-made meals. We want the harvest before we have tilled the soil and planted the seed.

Sometimes it is not just the nursing, tablets, injection or latest popular theory that makes the difference. Sometimes it's the kind words from a Nurse or Social Worker, friend or Service User that makes the difference.

For example, I was in a Mental Health hospital in Milton Keynes back in 1991 with Paranoid Schizophrenia, I was allowed out on for a few hours leave as part of my rehabilitation so I went to visit my local church. The voices I was experiencing would not leave me alone eventually someone asked me to leave the church if I could not behave. I do not think the voice asking me to leave came from the Priest, but I was distraught, I felt rejected, and devastated. Even God seemed to want nothing to do with me. The persecuting voices roared on.

When I got back to the Hospital, I found comfort in my fellow Service User, Ann, who simply came up to me and said "God is good!" She said this whenever she saw me and that's all she said, God is good, then she walked away. That was enough, it was enough to set me on the right path to recovery. Sometimes it is that simple. She made me feel good enough!

Ann saw a potential in me that others could not see; it is easier to spot potential when things are going well, but a lot more difficult when a person is experiencing Mental ill health. But acknowledgement of the Service User's potential and encouragement can literally be a life saver.

For instance, one of the feelings we might express when experiencing Mental ill health is: feeling useless, lack of hope for the future etc. By encouraging the Service User to work towards something they have always wanted to do and by the mere fact that you are prepared to take the Service User seriously, even if ultimately they do not achieve their goal. It can be enough that they explored the possibilities. This may be enough to start their new self belief building blocks for their future.

Another essential part of the Life Coaching G.R.O.W. Model is the "O" for options, sitting side by side with the Client/Service User looking at what options are available to them to choose, it can be so empowering for the Client/Service User, sheer advent of choice, brings with it hope. Hope being one of the essentials of empowering Recovery.

Often Client/Service Users discover options they never thought of before or reclaim opportunities they had once disregarded. As with my Client/Service User Tia, who set out to achieve something totally different to what she consciously perceived as necessary to achieve her goal of being more assertive. She decided she wanted to sing. By achieving her goal of singing she became more confident, thereby more assertive. Never in my wildest dreams can I say that I would have recommended singing as a vehicle to becoming assertive, but the Client/Service User often instinctively knows what they need. A parallel of this finding can be found in Person-Centred Counselling i.e. the Organismic Self.

The 7 elements of the Recovery Model based on Perkins and Repper.

1) Hope - this is described as the key to Recovery
2) A Secure base – appropriate Housing
3) Self - reclaiming the self that may have been taken away
4) Supportive relationships
5) Empowerment and inclusion
6) Coping strategies
7) Meaning

At best, modern day Psychiatry has really wanted to deal with coping strategies, that is strategies to help society cope, not the individual Service User. It just seems to want to keep the Service User in check i.e. control, restraint, over medication etc. The move towards the Recovery Model to my mind is cause for hope for future Service Users.

To be fair to Psychiatrists, sometimes, any good work they do is often undone by the demands of Society. For instance one can be on a Psychiatric ward and let's say for arguments sake that the treatment works. And let's suppose the Service User is suffering from depression and anxiety. The Service User comes home after being in Hospital. He or she is immediately faced by a pile of bills that could not be paid because they were in hospital and threatening phone calls from creditors, letters warning them of eviction and so on. Well you do not have to be be a brain surgeon to realise any work done by the Psychiatric system or even a good Psychologist is immediately destroyed. I do not believe in the nanny state, but a little care and a little common sense needs to prevail, or if you are an Accountant or Economist let me put it this way its a dreadful waste of resources both human and material resources.

Jigsaw puzzle

We are all part of the whole, we all interconnected, it is puzzling for me to see the medical profession trying to rush us Service Users through on a conveyor belt, when it is known to all that the medical approach is only one piece of the jigsaw. If we only focus on one part of the jigsaw we ignore the other pieces which complete the picture. It is like driving without glasses when you know you can hardly see without them; if you do get to your desired destination it's by accident.

The Factory belches out another solution whilst ignoring me, the Service User!

There are all manner of Recovery assessment Models to measure whether Recovery has taken place such as Milestones of Recovery (MOR), Recovery Enhancing Environment (REE), Recovery Measurement Tool (RMT), The Recovery Orientated System (ROSI), Stages of Recovery Instrument (STORI), etc.

I sometimes think that Professionals listen to the Service Users ideas then convert it into language that their Medical colleagues will understand, then it gets translated again for the Politicians. The Politicians subsequently convert it in to a complex legal document which becomes another rod for the back of the Service User; the original meaning and spirit of the initial consultation with the Service User being lost in translation and taken completely out of context.

I think it much more effective if the Nurse or Social Worker sat down over a cup of tea and biscuits and had a meaningful discussion rather than all these complicated tools, how can you be sure of their accuracy? Would you not have to ask the Service User if they feel they are Recovering?

Service Users for years asked if they could have paid work like their peers who had not experienced Mental ill health, they were very often denied this request by the Medical profession and Society itself which discriminated against those who had experienced Mental ill health; it was very difficult and is very difficult to get a job once one has acquired this label.

Nevertheless, Service Users pursued their mission through Charities like Rethink, Mind etc. All I am going to say is why are we being paraded as the villain of the peace? Like we did not want to work. Is this not emotional bullying? How does this help our Recovery?

Conservative Member of Parliament Philip Davies talks of people with disabilities being paid less than the minimum wage because they would find it easier to get employment. He also seemed to say in his address that he himself would not employ someone with a disability if he could get someone to do the job who did not have a disability. This is my understanding of what he said.

Treating disabled people as 2nd Class Citizens is appalling, Conservative MP Philip Davies seems to be targeting people with Mental health problems and/or those with Learning Difficulties, but does not himself encourage any prospective employers to look at the potential of persons with disabilities.

If reasonable adjustment had not been made for Stephen Hawkins the Scientist, who is confined to a wheelchair and has his speech aided by technology, would we be enjoying his theories? If reasonable adjustment had not been made for Douglas Bader the Battle of Britain RAF pilot, would we be here? If Tony Blair the former Prime Minister had excluded Alistair Campbell from his team in the Government would things have been different? Alistair Campbell has experienced Mental ill health but still held down the key job of Prime Minister's Director of Communications in spite of this from 1997 -2003.

Over the years people with Mental ill health have feared being locked up in Asylums or being excluded from society. Today it seems if you have Mental ill health you are best off not letting anyone know because of possible stigma. Parliament needs to put its own house in order and stop the emotional bullying!

Recovery is a journey, finding meaningful work may be helpful to that journey, setting Service Users up to fail is not.

Forcing Service Users to chase make believe jobs or degrading them by making them work for less than their fellow workers is just plain abuse. We want real jobs and not just glass collecting, since we have to live and pay our bills too!

One of the biggest aids to Recovery is respect, it ought to be pointed out that the Victorian age was great if you were rich, if you were poor God help you!

One in four British adults will experience Mental ill health at some time during their Lifetime according to the Office of National Statistics Psychiatric Mobility report 2001.

If we were to ask Members of Parliament and the House of Lords to publicly disclose whether they or any members of their family had ever experienced Mental ill health at any time, I do not believe many of them would do it. I am sure I would get shouts of the Hague trials, many would find it degrading. And thank God it is unethical to do such a thing, but is it o.k. to degrade our chances of finding meaningful work for decent pay by calling us scroungers?

If Parliament were to encourage Service Users to build up their self-esteem, instead of putting us down, they might actually find we are more valuable than they thought. A little respect and courtesy might save the nation billions of pounds.

What is the point of spending millions on the Time for Change project, which is about tackling stigma, if the very leaders of this Country do the very same thing that charities like Rethink are trying to change. All that effort and money wasted at a stroke of a pen. Suddenly Service Users are excluded once again.

A life with purpose and a meaningful life!

I sat in a dingy old bedsit, everything had gone, my wife, my step children, some good friends, the house, my job. Old battle scars reminded me of what I had lost, there seemed no point in living any longer, I was ready to put out the light in life for the last time. But something inside of me kept nudging me "you have not finished your work yet." I turned over and slept.

Oxleas Foundation Trust or Oxleas Trust as it was known then, had a very good branch called Opportunities which I was referred to by one of my previous Psychiatrists. They encouraged me and tried to help me find employment, which to me made the Locum Psychiatrist's letter stating that I was unlikely to work again, very strange. But that is water under the bridge now, it will not bring my family back to dwell on it.

Anyway, it was whilst I was with Opportunities that I developed the Personal Development course called "Building a Compelling Future", as I was determined to see my fellow Service User have a compelling future. This drive helped me to shape my life purpose which is to use my love, talents and abilities to coach others to build a compelling future!

Too often Service Users are marginalised, stigmatised, and their hopes and dreams crushed. I have been a Service User for 30 years and the only time I rally is when I do things in line with my purpose. Everyone in life has something they want to do, be or have, why not start working towards it today right here, right now!

When my fellow Service Users say they want to gain employment, I say if at all possible do something you love; another way of putting it is do not do it unless it makes your heart sing! Now that may seem irresponsible, but if we hate what we do, there is a greater chance of becoming ill again due to stress.

If the media is to be believed, people like Richard Branson and Paul McCartney, are so financially secure they need never work again, yet they keep working, why? Because they love what they do! It makes a difference. I suggest if we were all encouraged to do the things we love; the world would be a much less stressful place.

Often when one is suicidal, and I have experienced this myself, one will think to oneself what is the point? I have learned that if you have a sense of purpose you will know what the point is. Doing something you love will help you formulate that purpose.

A sense of purpose can lead us to a meaningful life.

"We must never forget that we may also find meaning in life even when confronted with a hopeless situation, when facing what cannot be changed. For what then matters is to bear witness to the uniquely human potential at its best, which is to transform a personal tragedy into a triumph, to turn one's predicament into human achievement."

From Man's Search for meaning by Victor Frankl. Published by Bacon Press (1959).

I just want to highlight the words "Uniquely human potential at its best, which is to transform a personal tragedy into a triumph" savour those words for a moment, look at the words potential and uniquely human; medicine should be about encouraging people like Service users to develop their own potential, there is more to being human than just their vital signs.

Often the Service User may experience more than it appears at face value, he or she may have lost their job, have broken relationships, lost friendships, lost their home etc. These things may have been the very pillars of their lives and there may be no chance of getting them back. They might well ask themselves; what is the point? Amongst this avalanche of pain it is helpful if one has a sense of purpose, having a sense of purpose can lead to meaning; let me try to illustrate the point.

Dr Victor Frankl who wrote the book: "Man's Search for meaning" was arrested along with his wife and family, and taken to Theresienstadt a Concentration camp in 1942. Dr Victor Frankl lost everyone except for his little sister who managed to escape to Australia. When the Russian Army liberated Theresienstadt in 1945 there were only 17,247 survivors out of the 144,000 Jews that had been sent to the Concentration camp.

Despite the human tragedy caused by Nazi Germany Dr Victor Frankl found meaning by pursing his interest in Psychology which was part of his purpose. He was able to observe and make the following discovery of what he was to call Logo therapy by asking the following question "How can one say yes to life, despite tragedy and suffering?" By helping patients to answer this question for themselves and find meaning in their experiences, Dr Frankl was also able to find meaning to his own experiences. If we are going to help Service Users Recover we have got to encourage hope, meaning and the possibility of triumph over adversity.

Recovery is like water it can take many shapes and guises, when placed in a bowl it can take the shape of that bowl, if placed in glass or a bath it can take those shapes. Water can be a babbling brook or raging waterfall, in all its shapes and forms it is teeming with life. Sometimes the Life in the water, that includes even the tinniest droplet, is unseen by the naked eye. The Service user's Recovery is like that droplet of water, something unique and special. Yet like the water in the bowl or in the waterfall they are part of a whole. Like the scientists who established that there are life forms that are unseen to the naked eye, by using tools such as Microscopes, so too; should Health Professionals and the like be encouraged to see Service Users' potential not just their medical symptoms. Then maybe, just maybe; they can evoke a sense of hope!

Chapter 7

Ask the Coach - Questions and Answers

Is it really that simple or is there more to Coaching than just the G.R.O.W. Model?

Yes, the G.R.OW. Model really is that simple, but it is necessary to develop Coaching skills i.e. building rapport, being able to listen, being able to challenge limiting beliefs and so on. However, this is beyond the scope of this book but I do recommend The Coaching Academy as Coach Trainers.

In applying for Life Coaching to Mental health what happens if a patient is sectioned and the Health professionals feel that patient would benefit from Life Coaching, but the patient does not want to do it. Can they be forced to do it?

The simple answer is NO! When a patient is sectioned they are there against their will under the Mental Health act 1983, under for instance section 2, or 3. Normally because they may be a risk to themselves or others. But the whole purpose of Life Coaching that I practice is that to be effective, Life Coaching must be done with the Service Users or patients consent at all times, even if they are under a section at the time of having Life Coaching. Not unlike Counsellors who practice Person-Centred Counselling where consent is a pre-condition of Counselling. Should the Service User withdraw their consent at any time the Coaching session must come to a halt.

Can Life Coaching be used on the wards of a Mental Hospital?

I believe it can, but I cannot say I have achieved this to a satisfactory level. There is great suspicion by patients of everybody and a deep concern about confidentiality. It also depends on which ward the Service Users are in, some are far more intense than others. Note It must be a given, when working on the wards, that you always have the permission of the Hospital.

However, from a practical point of view it is easier for Client/Service Users to access resources when they are in the community as the Client/Service User is encouraged to do their own research and may be asked by their Coach to complete certain tasks. It is very difficult for a Service User to do this whilst on the ward since there may be certain restrictions e.g. they may not be able to keep an appointment because they have been told they have to attend ward round, or they may not have free access to a Computer or Library. Life Coaching is about encouraging the Client/Service User to access existing resources too!

Can Life Coaching only be used for Recovery?

In my opinion the Service User in Recovery is the best point to use Life Coaching with regards to Mental Health. Because during the deep onset of the illness the Service User may find it difficult to respond to or complete tasks set by the Coach.

Where Coaching and Mental Health is concerned is there any advantage in having a Life Coach who is a Service User over a Non Service User Life Coach?

The main advantage is that the Service User Life Coach would be able to identify with the Client/Service User from a Service User Perspective; the Service User Life Coach has experience that money cannot buy, for they have already been in the desert and hopefully found the trail out.

Can other Professionals other than Health Professionals use Life Coaching e.g. Social Workers?

Definitely, yes.

Imagine visiting your client and after you have gone through the necessary procedures like risk assessment etc. You ask them sincerely if they have any goals or what they would really like to do be or have? Maybe you could help them come up with a short list, that alone could help their self-esteem.

So often Service Users are told what they cannot do or cannot have. Then imagine you are empowering them to work toward their goal; this gives a whole different outlook to life itself, it may even instil in the Client/Service User a whole new sense of purpose.

What about Life Coaching and Medication?

Life Coaching is not designed to take the place of any medication and I would advise any Client/Service User to consult their medical team before coming off medication. As I have stated previously, I take medication but I find Life Coaching like Counselling or Relaxation techniques especially helpful working alongside my medication therapy. So it is what works for the individual, there is no one cap fits all.

What would you do if the Client/Service User is taken seriously ill in your session?

If you are really worried, call an Ambulance! Like any ordinary citizen would; as you only have the same rights as any ordinary civilian.

What would you do if the client said they were suicidal?

If I were seriously worried I would remind them of my confidential policy which is "Everything is confidential unless you are likely to harm yourself or others" and immediately call for an Ambulance.

Can working for an organisation effect the Life Coaches' confidentiality policy?

Yes it can but it depends on the agreement thrashed out between the Coach and the organisation, which is why I believe it is important to tell the client what the confidentiality policy is, from the outset.

Can Life Coaching work with any diagnosis?

I do not know since I do not ask my Client/Service Users what their diagnosis is, since there is no reason for me to know, unless they choose to tell me. I work with the person before me, not the diagnosis, besides I am not trying to bring about a medical cure but trying to effect transition.

Is there anything you as a Life Coach would not do?

There are many things I would not do, but I feel it is important for me to state that I would NOT knowingly assist or help a Client Service User to commit Suicide. Apart from the fact that it is illegal, one never knows what tomorrow will bring and I can testify to that. There have been occasions when I have attempted suicide; yet I am here today encouraging my fellow Service Users to reach out for a better quality of life. "Yes you can!"

How do you know Life Coaching works?

Firstly through personal experience of being Coached as a Service User. Secondly, by the results my client's say they have achieved. Ask your client's if it works. See the Client/Service User revel in their successes! Then ask yourself does it work?

The good thing about this style of Life Coaching is, using the G.R.O.W. Model the Client/Service User says from the start what he or she would like to achieve. This enables both the Client/Service User and the Coach to mark the target that is the result they desire to achieve, thereby dispelling any coded smoke signals and making it easier for both the Client/Service User and the coach to assess whether the Coaching is working.

Chapter 8

Service User in the Driving Seat

Notice I did not say or use the words "put" or "let" the Service User in the driving seat. No! I believe the Service User has the right to take the driver's seat of his or her life. After all whose life is it anyway? That is not to say that Service Users will never use the skills and tools of Professionals to reach the destination that they, the Service User have chosen.

Often when one buys a car one may have it serviced by a Mechanic, one may have it spray painted, or an exhaust fitted, but that does not mean one is not the driver. Generally speaking the driver/owner hires and fires who works on his or her car and certainly as a driver they set the compass as to the direction they wish to travel. Or should I say plots the course on their Satellite Navigator.

I believe Coaching is just like the Satellite Navigator where the Client/Service User can choose and chart the direction they want to take. It is not that Service Users will never need Nurses, Doctors, Psychiatrists, Social Workers and the like, but they should be able to choose when and how they work with them whilst they are in Recovery.

This idea is no more radical than the idea that a person in Court has the right to choose whether or not he wants to have a Lawyer. In some cases the person's very life may have depended on it i.e. when Capital Punishment was legal. Why then do we say that Service Users in Recovery cannot choose how they will affect their Recovery. You never know the person standing before the Gallows may be innocent, the Service User may have found a better way to regain their health; after all Professionals get it wrong sometimes too, don't they?

I refer to Prisoners being victims of miscarriages of Justice, I think of Grieving Mothers who were sent to Prison having been convicted of killing their Babies; as in Sally Clarke's case 1965 -2007 see article by Jamie Downward in Guardian 18th March 2007 or Baby P. case see article "Treated like a dog, used as a punch bag the life and death of a baby called smiley." written by Vanessa Allen and Colin Fernandez from Mail online 11th September 2011 or Christopher Clunis see article called "The Clunis case passing the buck carried on until an innocent man died." By Rosie Waterhouse and Rhys Williams taken from the Independent Newspaper 19th July 1983. In that article it was said that in February 1988 Christopher Clunis "frequently turned up at the Chase Farm Casualty Department, either because police referred him there or he took himself there, because he was homeless." I would suggest that Christopher Clunis came to Casualty as a cry for help. Sometimes the Service user does know best. Listen and hear!

WHO DARES TO CARE?

My fellow Service Users and friends of Service Users, Family, also the Carers, Doctors Nurses, Psychiatrists, Social Workers, plus all the unsung heroes who got into action to help us Service Users in our times of need. I take my hat off to you with the utmost respect. Anyone, including myself, can be an armchair critic. At the end of the day you dared to care, you tried to make a difference, often working within restrictive frameworks. Let not my sharp criticisms deflate you, at least open your hearts and minds to new ways of doing things, if not this way then another, always work alongside the Service user as we all have different needs. Do not shout from your lofty Towers, puffed up with self pride, get alongside. For we are all human and we all make mistakes, me included. If everyone has the answer to Mental ill health how comes we are still talking about the revolving door syndrome? I do not have the answer, but I may have one piece of the jigsaw puzzle.

OUT OF THE MOUTHS OF BABES.

I remember being told this story in Church a few years back. A Minister in his study was trying to write Sundays Sermon, his wife had just popped out to see a friend leaving his young son in his care. The son kept on interrupting him as he tried to write his Sermon. The Minister became so exasperated that in a huff he got up and picked a magazine and opened it to some complicated words which he knew his son could never work out and tore the page from the magazine. He then gave it to his son and said there, see if you can put this puzzle together. The son looked at the piece of paper which was once a page in a magazine and got to work. The Minister breathed a sigh of relief as he soldiered on with his Sermon assuming his son would be occupied with the puzzle for some time.

Within 4 minutes his son shouted finished. The Minister walked over to his son and to his amazement he had completed the puzzle. The Minister asked his son how he had completed the puzzle so quickly.

The son explained, on the opposite of the complicated words was a picture of a man's face so he turned it over and put the picture together, thus causing the complicated words to fit together solving the puzzle. The Minister smiled at his clever son as he now had the material for his Sermon.

The moral of the story is sometimes the untrained mind can find a better way. I conclude, if you let the Service user picture the way they would like to live their lives and choose their own goals, then sustained Recovery will be more likely. Life Coaching maybe another jigsaw piece!

Keynote Speech:

DON'T PARK YOUR DREAMS, DRIVE 'EM!

Take a deep breath and pause for a moment. What are you thinking? May be you are thinking life has not been kind to you, may be you are thinking you are to blame for things that have gone wrong in your life, maybe someone else is to blame.

I used to run Drop-in Centres for those who like myself have experienced Mental ill health. The Drop-ins were based in Milton Keynes and were set up by the National Schizophrenia Fellowship (now called ReThink). Sometimes I would run small discussion groups in the Drop-in.

What amazed me was that whenever I asked what made them happy, I would only get an occasional reply; then silence. But if I asked what made them sad I would get a list long enough to wrap round the Empire State building 3 times. How comes we always know what makes us unhappy? And before you say it is because they are unwell, it also seems that this true of the general public too.

I suggest you take another deep breath and pause for a moment think of things in your life you either felt or feel happy about. It could be your first kiss, your first beer, your first pair of long trousers or maybe you have a few dreams to live, maybe there is something you want to do, be, or have. What are you waiting for?

What are you waiting for?

Now there's a question

Are you waiting for the perfect moment?

Are you waiting until everything falls into place?

Are you waiting to be discovered?

Are you waiting for that Lottery win?

Well there are plenty of people waiting in the queue, so if you do not want to wait forever make your dreams happen! Get started and start working towards your dreams; you will be surprised who will come along and give you a hand.

Then hopefully, you will have more of the things that brings you happiness in your life.

WHY PUT YOUR DREAMS ON HOLD?

DON'T PARK YOUR DREAMS DRIVE 'EM !

ACTION NOW; IS A LIFE IN PROGRESS!

Moot point: the word empowerment has largely been absent from this book. I want you to ask yourself the following: does it only count as empowerment if the Service User does what the Professional wants or sticks to the Professional's plan?

I then want you to consider this quote from Thomas Edison, who amongst other things invented the Light bulb and the Phonograph, he said:

"Just because something does not do what we planned it to do, does not mean it's useless."

Discuss.

The W. in the G.R.O.W. Model that I use stands for willingness to act. This asks the question: are you prepared to pay the price (this does not necessarily refer to money) to reach your dream or goal? I contend that the Service User is more willing to act or if you like is more motivated to achieve his or her goal or dream if it is something he or she wants to do.

Society tends to write people off, because they are not doing, or not able to do, what Society has planned for them to do. But like Thomas Edison says that does not mean they're useless. Our greatest Heroes and Heroines did things differently or had a different view on life to what was the norm of society in those particular time slots. Thomas Edison is a fine example of this.

Life Coaching is extremely action orientated. One can do all the wishing and chewing over theories one likes, but without taking the necessary action steps one might as well curl up on the settee with the Television remote control or watch Goldfish swimming around the Goldfish bowl. No! Life Coaching is proactive, it is about taking responsibility and achieving your own goals, it is about taking action. That is not to say one will always achieve one's goal, there is always the risk you may not, but the odds are far greater against you not achieving your goal if you do not take action; one just does the best one can.

In the 1960's I had heard of people like the Hurdler David Hemmings, and Lyn Davies the Long Jumper but I had never heard of the Paralympics. This is where people with disabilities compete in their own Olympics.

Back in the 1960's this must have seemed like just a pipe dream to many, yet today it is just seen as part of the natural order of things.

We never know what tomorrow will bring.

Does a sailor know exactly which way the wind will blow or where it comes from? He or she may make estimates using their experience or the latest technology; but if our weather forecasts are anything to go by we are not there yet.

The Boy Scouts have it right "BE PREPARED."

Make sure you have taken the necessary steps to build your boat if you want to get to the other side of the river.

Inaction can be a killer.

Failure to take action is not only a dream stealer it can be a killer. For there is one thing worse than having no dreams at all and that is failing to take action to make one's dreams happen.

I believe Alcoholism, depression etc. can sometimes be exacerbated by feelings caused by failure to take action steps, how often have you heard the words "If only I had done this or that?" Or I wasted my opportunity because I'd not done this or that?"

Moot: Point: Does Mental illness exist or is it simply a case of broken dreams?

Most people in Society seem to admire those who have a great bias for action, they seem to have a "why not now?" approach to life.

Olympic Athletes often train for years before they achieve their dream of becoming Olympic Champions. They will usually start training whilst they are Schoolchildren with nothing more than a hope or a dream to drive them, then it manifests a dream and then a reality. To achieve their dream these Athletes will often be training early in the morning, whilst many of us are tucked up in bed and late into the night when many of us are squinting at the television. Heroes and heroines like Daly Thompson, Sebastian Coe, or Dame Kelly Holmes. We can also look to businessmen, Actors, and Scientists who have often worked long and hard to achieve their dreams.

So get started don't be misled by the myth of the overnight success or the should have done it by now brigade. Remember the story of the Hare and the Tortoise in Aesop's Fables, which shows that consistent right action over came the flurry of the Hare in a Hurry. Think Kaizen, that is take small quality steps.

One can often challenge the notion that one is too old or too young to do something, look at Boris Becker who was age 17 when he won his first Wimbledon title or Ronald Regan America's oldest President or even Evelyn "Nana" Gregory who at the age of 71 made History by becoming the oldest person ever to be hired as a flight attendant. Being a flight attendant had been her childhood dream which she to managed to achieve with Mesa Airlines.

Post to Post, Goal to Goal.

The thing about the Tortoise in Aesop's Fable is the Tortoise was playing to his own strengths, taking slow consistent action and did not worry about the opposition. The Tortoise used his gift of perseverance to outsmart the lightening speed of the Hare. When you are running post to post or from point to point at least estimate how far you have to run, that is plan your journey. Do not be caught out like the Hare; out of puff.

When you have achieved your Goal, move on to another, for everything that lives is in perpetual motion.

GOAL ON!

Life Coaching is just another well meaning theory or model unless you, the Client/Service User takes action, it is like that dusty old book of wisdom that you never read and when the Teacher asks you if you have read it. You say no, but I have got the book. Whilst thoughtful, consistent right action means the Goal is on!

CREATING FUTURE HISTORY

The Master of creating future history is Mohammed Ali the former World Heavy Weight Boxing Champion. He used to picture or visualize exactly how he wanted the fight to go and how he wanted it to end up. Very often Mohammed Ali would end up the victor having predicted the exact round in which he would win the fight. For a long time Mohammed Ali (formerly known as Cassius Clay) was thought to be unbeatable, if anyone says visualization does not work tell them to talk to the Greatest: Mohammed Ali.

I bring creating future history up for two reasons: firstly, for me Life Coaching is about empowering the Client/Service User to create future history. It starts with the end game or goal the client requires. In short, where do they want to end up? So often people start their journey without a notion of where they want to end up. They just ramble through life with no particular place to go. If that's you're objective it's O.K. But don't complain if you don't know where you are in life. Life Coaching is about using the G,R.O.W. Model and asks firstly where do you want to end up? What do you want? What is your desired goal?

The second point is that Life Coaching is not just about merely solving problems but creating future history. Often when one points the boat in the direction one wants to go, one often ends up solving other problems by default or manage them better.

Introducing Premila Trivedi, who has worked in a range of projects both Statutory and Third Sector Agencies and was employed for 5 years as a Service User Education & Training Advisor at The South London and Maudsley Hospital NHS Trust. She has written many chapters and articles for various Mental health books, and is a Service User.

Premila says "(Mental health) Services often put you back to where you were before you had a crash, maybe to the position that caused the crash – sometimes this recreates the problem."

Premila is talking about The Services tendency to want to examine the past, sometimes when you have fallen down a hole it is wise to stop digging and start climbing out and head towards the light. There is a time for lamenting and a time for moving on!

Introducing John Crowley, who is an NHS Mental health Nurse and

Senior Lecturer with The University of Greenwich.

John says "going back 20 years, then the Professionals actively asked the Service User to give up work – not a good idea. We have changed a lot now!"

What would have happened had the Services Users been able to follow their own paths? Who knows?

John also highlights the need for self-esteem and how much easier it is to build on a one-to-one basis.

"There are clients; if distressed; self esteem is low it is easier in a one to one basis than in a group."

It is easier to be flexible around a clients needs if the Coaching is one to one by giving privacy to the client they are much more likely to disclose their personal goals.

One thing I learned is I had to take ownership, if things went belly up it was down to me but also the reverse is true, if I am successful it was down to me. As in the tittle of Larry Winget's book called "Success is your own damn fault." It really grates with me when Mentors say "I made you." As Coaching clients we have got to own our own successes thus building our own self-esteem.

PANORAMIC VIEW OF CREATING FUTURE HISTORY.

I am hoping that Life Coaching will become a widely used tool in the Medical Profession and with Personalisation Budgets looming I predict that the Health Service will have to have a more positive focus. People are not going to pay for more doom and gloom if Service Users are not satisfied with the Service they won't pay for it. I also hope Social Workers and other ancillary workers take advantage of using Life Coaching with their clients too.

I especially hope that Service Users, having had appropriate Life Coaching Training will also take up the mantle and Coach themselves and others where appropriate.

Ke note Speech:

CREATING FUTURE HISTORY

You do not need an alibi for your life, no excuses, no back stage passes required. So live it 'cause you own it, and do the best you can.

We all make mistakes, if I cried for every mistake I have made, the Universe would not be big enough to hold my tears. Pssss! Anyone who has never made a mistake has never done anything.

Face your day be proud to be you, acknowledge your mistakes but above all celebrate your successes whether they be small, large, or indifferent. Every success helps, every success counts.

Everyone loves a winner, but stand by yourself when the crowd has thinned because you did not win. Love yourself no matter what!

Make sure that time does not catch you waiting for an alibi, for life is not a rehearsal, it is the real thing. So puff out your cheeks with air, take a deep breath and live like the champion you are!

Write Your Own Epilogue!

Write your own epilogue or post script as to how Life Coaching has influenced you, or your clients. Notice the difference between before and after Life Coaching listing the things you have achieved.

You will be amazed.

Take the time to list in this space below how Life Coaching has influenced your life:

WHAT HAPPENS NEXT IS UP TO YOU!

Thank You

I would like to say a special thank you to all the Service Users and Professionals plus my friends and family who have given me encouragement in writing this book.

In particular I would like to thank

Garry Ellison

Kayin

Mary Hernandez

Tia

For sharing their experience of Life Coaching with us.

I would also like to thank my Mentors Mr Fabians Best and the late
Mrs Jean Wickson.

Finally, thank you the reader for taking the time to read my book.

About the Author

Humphrey A. Greaves
Professional Life Coach and NLP Practitioner

Humphrey Greaves has been using the Mental health Services since 1981 he is currently a Professional Life Coach and has had his own Coaching Practice since 2002.

Humphrey has also previously worked as a Project Worker for the National Schizophrenia Fellowship running Drop Ins, Employment Advisor (Mental Health) for Shaw Trust, BME User Development Worker for Southwark Mind where Humphrey now works as a Freelance Professional Life Coach.

Humphrey has written a song called Mental illness ain't Choosey hich was played on 3 Counties Radio in 1996 more recently has been a contributing author to the book "Mental health; Service User Involvement and Recovery Edited by Jenny Weinstein (Published by Jessica Kingsley Publishing 2010) Humphrey has also appeared on BBC Radio 4 program "All in the MIND"

Humphrey Greaves Coaching Practice can be found at:

www.hgreavescoaching.netlinux.co.uk

Tel 07535641443

Email: humphreygreaves@gmail.com

Printed in Great Britain
by Amazon